Children Non-Fiction
j 940.5318 Y8

Handler, Andrew, 1935-
Young people speak : surviving the Holocaust in Hungary /

9000738531

D1801057

C
Children's Room
Mead Public Library
Sheboygan, Wisconsin

Borrowers are responsible for all library materials drawn on their cards and for all charges accruing on same.

DEMCO

YOUNG PEOPLE SPEAK
SURVIVING THE HOLOCAUST
IN HUNGARY

YOUNG PEOPLE SPEAK
SURVIVING THE HOLOCAUST IN HUNGARY

Compiled and edited by
ANDREW HANDLER
and
SUSAN V. MESCHEL

FRANKLIN WATTS
New York • Chicago • London • Toronto • Sydney

IN MEMORY OF
DR. JOHN STRASSER,
TEACHER AND FRIEND

Photographs courtesy of the authors

Library of Congress Cataloging-in-Publication Data

Young people speak : surviving the Holocaust in Hungary / compiled by
Andrew Handler and Susan Meschel.
p.   cm.
Includes bibliographical references and index.
Summary: Eleven survivors of the Holocaust in Hungary recollect
their childhood experiences during the implementation of Hitler's
Final Solution.
ISBN 0-531-11044-3
1. Jews—Hungary—Biography—Juvenile literature. 2. Holocaust,
Jewish (1939–1945)—Hungary—Personal narratives—Juvenile
literature. 3. Jewish children—Hungary—Biography—Juvenile
literature. 4. Hungary—Biography—Juvenile literature.
[1. Holocaust, Jewish (1939–1945)—Hungary—Personal narratives.
2. Jews—Hungary—Biography.] I. Handler, Andrew, 1935–   .
II. Meschel, Susan. III. Title: Surviving the Holocaust in Hungary.
DS135.H93A18   1993
940.53′18′0922—dc20
[B]
92-41701 CIP AC

Copyright © 1993 by Andrew Handler and Susan V. Meschel
All rights reserved
Printed in the United States of America
6 5 4 3 2 1

CONTENTS

PREFACE 7

INTRODUCTION 9

WE PRETEND
GABOR KALMAN 19

I AM NOT GOING!
PETER O. MILCH 27

BECAUSE I WANTED TO BE AN OLYMPIC CHAMPION
ÉVA SZÉKELY 41

LET THOSE WHO STEAL A CHILDHOOD BE PUNISHED
MARTHA HENTZ 51

MY BRIEFCASE
ANDREW HANDLER 57

THE BEGINNING OF THE END
SUSAN V. MESCHEL 67

THE BRICKYARD
PETER BARTA   85

HAVE YOU EVER MADE A WHISTLE OF AN APRICOT PIT?
TIBOR BAUER   95

THANK YOU, RAOUL WALLENBERG
PETER TARJAN   115

DO YOU BELIEVE IN MIRACLES?
GEORGE S. PICK   123

THE BIRTHDAY SURPRISE
ANDRÉ STEIN   141

FOR FURTHER READING
158

INDEX
159

PREFACE

The contributors to this anthology have three unique characteristics in common. First, all of them were children during the Second World War and thus belong to the last generation of survivors who were old enough to be aware of the sights and sounds of the Holocaust. They recall their experiences with the firm ring of authenticity. Second, all of them were born and brought up in Hungary, the country that was the last to be occupied by Hitler's armies and the one that witnessed the quickest implementation of the Final Solution. Between April 1944 and January 1945 more than 75 percent of Hungarian Jewry perished—approximately 600,000 people. Third, none of the contributors relates experiences in extermination camps, which constitute the majority of survivor accounts in Holocaust literature. Instead, they revisit and again walk such roads to survival as living in the ghetto, attempting to avoid being caught and deported, and adjusting to a life in hiding or under an assumed name.

Although they existed virtually from hour to hour and agonized over the sufferings and deaths of loved ones, the authors as children faced every dangerous situation and unpredictable turn of events with ingenuity and fortitude, hope and optimism. In the shadow of destruction there was even occasion to smile at the comic fortuity of fate. The sight or remembrance of precious toys, exuberantly played games, favorite foods, and familiar faces and places brought brief periods of joy to a world of deprivations.

The editors wish to express their appreciation to the contributors for their resolve and labor. The painful experience of reliving horrifying times of their childhood, often reopening wounds that cannot heal, was compensated by the hope that their recollections would help add new pieces to the mosaic of the Holocaust.

INTRODUCTION

The war in Europe had been raging for five years. By early 1945 the land had been laid waste, many cities destroyed and millions of people made homeless, wounded, or killed. The gray-green–uniformed soldiers of the Third Reich who had marched with such self-assurance on the wide boulevards of Paris and prepared with hate-filled resolve to capture Leningrad were now fighting for a lost cause. Yet, instead of generals slowly giving way to diplomats in the honorable tradition of transferring action from the battlefield to the conference table, the fighting dragged on, at times and in places more desperately than ever before. Hitler's obsession with world conquest, his desire for a world dominated by racially pure Germans, and his belief in a miracle weapon that would turn things around cost hundreds of thousands of lives that could have been spared. In April 1945, Allied soldiers had to fight from street to street and house to house until they reached Hitler's bunker in Berlin around which the last defenders of the Third Reich, many of them teenage members of the Hitler Youth organization, fought and died. On May 7, 1945, the war in Europe ended. By then six million Jews—children, parents, and grandparents—had also perished. They did not die fighting on battlefields or in cities bombed by warplanes but in crowded ghettos and sprawling concentration camps. Also, many men—sons and fathers, nephews and uncles—went to certain death serving in forced labor battalions. Hitler's Final Solution of the Jewish Question—extermination of the Jews—however, was no more successful than his plan to become master of the world. The memory of the victims of the Holocaust is kept alive by those whose very lives are reminders of the fallacy and futility of the will to hate and to exterminate.

In the midst of fighting and destruction there was an island of relative tranquility: Hungary. Although Hungarians had contributed their share to keeping anti-Semitism alive through the centuries, they stopped short of working out their own version of the Final Solution. Since 1867, when Jews were emancipated and put on an equal footing with the rest of the citizens of the country, the Hungarian government had safeguarded their rights and recognized their economic and cultural contributions. Many Hungarian Jews fought with distinction and died or were wounded in the battles of World War I. Some even received titles of nobility.

There was an upsurge of anti-Jewish activities after World War I. A Soviet-style dictatorship, whose leaders included some of Jewish origin, was set up in March 1919. Anti-Communist forces destroyed it within three months. Bands of right-wing army officers combed the countryside in search of real and imagined sympathizers of the hated Communist regime. In parts of Hungary Jews were beaten, tortured, and murdered.

Conditions improved, and the threat to Jews eased for the better part of the interwar period. Admiral Miklós Horthy, who became regent of Hungary in 1920, succeeded in keeping the forces of anti-Semitism at bay. Although he did not prevent the anti-Semites from establishing political parties and making inflammatory speeches in the Hungarian Parliament, Horthy ruled with an iron hand and insisted on maintaining law and order. Jews were allowed to participate in all sectors of Hungarian social, economic, and cultural life.

After neighboring Austria was annexed by Nazi Germany in March 1938, great pressure was put on Horthy to initiate anti-Jewish legislation. Two months later the first anti-Jewish laws were passed in Parliament; others were passed in May 1939 and July 1942. As a result, the systematical elimination of Jews from economic and cultural pursuits began. Jews were increasingly deprived of their legal equality. The Jewish religion, which had been made equal to all other faiths fifty years earlier, was also made illegal. Jewish athletes were excluded from sports clubs and competition. In the countryside, Jews were assaulted and ostracized. The Hungarian authorities declared that they would proceed to effect the orderly and legal solution of the Jewish Question.

The fate of Hungarian Jewry seemed sealed. Suddenly the impossible happened. In March 1942, Horthy appointed as prime minister Miklós Kállay, a member of the nobility and a foe of both the Nazis and their Hungarian sympathizers, the members of the Arrow Cross Party. Both Horthy and Kállay insisted that Hungary would retain the right as a sovereign state to resolve the Jewish Question independent of foreign influences. Hungary's economy, they declared, would collapse if the Jews were excluded from it.

For two years, while much of the rest of European Jewry in countries under German rule fell victim to the Nazis' Final Solution, Hungarian Jews did not even have to wear the yellow cloth Star of David. Nor did they have to fear being deported, made to live in designated quarters, or herded into the dreaded cattle cars that would speed in the direction of Auschwitz or some other destination that the Nazis had made infamous.

Horthy and Kállay kept Hitler, then preoccupied with the invasion of the Soviet Union, at bay by arguing that Hungary had to retain control of its internal affairs if it were to remain a useful ally of Germany. They did accede to some of his demands without giving up significant ground. Some restrictions were imposed on the Jews, but they merely caused inconvenience for them in comparison with the tragedy that befell Jews elsewhere.

Before the war Jews had moved freely in all sectors of Hungary's economy and culture, but now their lives centered on the Jewish community and its many institutions. Jewish schools and sports clubs, culture halls where plays, operas, and concerts were presented, and Jewish newspapers, magazines, and books experienced a flurry of activity and creativity. On March 19, 1944, the bubble burst. German troops poured across the border and occupied Hungary. No longer willing to put up with his ally's policies, Hitler decided to impose his will on the small hapless neighbor of the Third Reich. Kállay fled to the Turkish embassy but was subsequently arrested and interned.

Hungarians were no longer the masters of their country—the Nazis were. Two days after the Germans occupied Hungary, Adolf Eichmann, who was the chief Nazi organizer of transporting Jews to the various concentration and extermination camps, arrived in Budapest. The government ordered all Jews to wear the "Jew's star," the six-pointed Star of David made of yellow cloth, sewn over the left side of the outer garment, readily visible in public.

On May 14 the deportation of Jews from the countryside began. Supervised by Hungarian policemen and gendarmes (rural police) whose cruelty surpassed even that of the Nazis, nearly half a million Jews boarded crowded death trains and were transported to Auschwitz, Mauthausen, and Buchenwald. By the summer of 1944 the Hungarian countryside was virtually devoid of Jews, or as the Germans were fond of saying, *Judenrein*.

On June 24 the government of General Döme Sztójay, a known admirer of the Nazis who had succeeded Kállay as prime minister, ordered the Jews of Budapest to leave their homes and move into 2,600 large apartment houses marked with the six-pointed star in the central district of the capital.

INTRODUCTION

The end of the remnant of Hungary's once large Jewish community seemed within sight. The ghetto was known to be the antechamber of death. The inhabitants were to die or be killed there or held until transported to extermination camps. A few days later thousands of gendarmes, who had committed some of the most brutal atrocities against the Jews in the countryside, arrived in Budapest. Rumors about a coup by right-wing extremists quickly spread in the city. However, after a firm order from the regent and a show of force by Hungarian troops rushed to Budapest, the gendarmes departed. Still, nothing could deter Eichmann from putting the wheels of his infamous death trains in motion. On July 8, 25,000 Jews were put on board and transported to extermination camps. Hitler sent a personal message to Horthy in which he insisted that all Jews in Budapest be deported. Plans were drawn up to start their removal on August 27 and complete it within three weeks. Naturally the inhabitants of the star-marked houses braced themselves for the worst. It looked as if an avalanche of hatred and fanaticism was about to bury its helpless victims. Suddenly the avalanche came to a screeching halt.

Only top Hungarian and German officials knew that Horthy had been trying to replace pro-Nazi Prime Minister Sztójay since early July. Conditions were unfavorable, and Horthy found no one brave and reliable enough to steer the helm of Hungarian politics and life. Within two months, however, pressure tactics that had been directed against Germany for some time began to show results in Hungary. The War Refugee Board, created by an order of President Roosevelt in January 1944, was empowered to negotiate with the Nazis directly about ways of rescuing the remnants of European Jewry from the Final Solution. It threatened with severe punishment those who participated in the practice of genocide or cooperated with the Nazis. The Vatican, under pressure from the United States and neutral countries, began denouncing the atrocities and those who committed them. The Vatican permitted such princes of the Church as Cardinal

Roncalli, who later became Pope John XXIII, to engage in rescue efforts. The International Red Cross abandoned its policy of not becoming involved in matters outside its realm of competence. In addition, the massive air attacks on the capitals and principal cities of the Third Reich and its allies caused widespread consternation among leading politicians and the military. As a result, by the summer of 1944 statements were made by Hitler and by Heinrich Himmler—the head of the SS (elite guard) and the principal organizer of the Final Solution—about technical difficulties in completing the destruction of European Jewry. Gradually the rescue efforts grew bolder.

Individual acts of heroism—such as those attributed to Raoul Wallenberg, a secretary of the Swedish embassy in Budapest, and representatives of other neutral nations and the Vatican who issued documents of protection and transformed leased buildings into safe houses—saved the lives of thousands of Jews. But Eichmann, obsessed with the meticulous performance of his duties, persisted. He organized new shipments of human cargo to the extermination camps, often evading or countermanding the orders of his superiors.

Detecting the winds of change, Horthy made his move. On August 28 the regent forced Prime Minister Sztójay to resign and named General Géza Lakatos, the former commander of the First Hungarian Army and no admirer of the Nazis, to head a military government. The new prime minister ordered the infamous freight trains to halt, and Eichmann quickly slipped out of Hungary on August 29th. "With regard to the Jewish Question," Lakatos declared, "procedures in the strictest conformity with the laws are being put into effect that will insure that the most harmful elements and the unemployed are put to useful work." To the nearly 200,000 Jews in the ghetto of Budapest, Lakatos's words sounded like a miracle in the making.

The miracle lasted only six weeks. Horthy's appointment of Lakatos angered Hitler. The Nazi dictator grew weary of his Hungarian ally, accusing Horthy of dishonesty and duplicity. The charges were not unfounded. Stunned by the defections of Rumania, Bulgaria, and Finland from their alliance with Germany and anguished by the steadily advancing Soviet armies, Horthy secretly sent negotiators to Moscow on September 28. Nearly two weeks of talks followed. On October 11, the regent's envoys signed an agreement pledging that Hungarian troops would withdraw from territories they had occupied and would be placed at the disposal of the Soviet Union.

Horthy's intentions were good, albeit belated. Only his calculations proved inaccurate. Convinced he enjoyed the loyalty of the Hungarian armed forces, Horthy decided to take his country out of the war, which he felt Germany had already lost. On October 15 he read a brief proclamation on the Hungarian radio, announcing an end to the hostilities. Peace in Hungary, however, lasted only for hours. The Germans, aided by pro-Nazi Hungarian army officers and extreme right-wing politicians, seized Horthy's son and had the proclamation declared unconstitutional by an intimidated Parliament. Horthy had gambled and lost. The Germans forced him to sign a document of resignation, and he and his family were taken into protective custody and transported to Germany.

The new masters of Hungary were Ferenc Szálasi and his Arrow Cross Party. The Arrow Cross leader wanted to place the insignia of his movement—two arrows, with arrowheads on all four tips, intersecting each other in the middle—next to the Nazi swastika, making them the symbols of the co-creators of a new National Socialist Europe. Like Hitler, Szálasi was an avowed racist. His utopia called for a Great Fatherland inhabited by racially pure Hungarians. It was on the subject of Jews that Szálasi and Hitler differed. Whereas anti-Semitism was a cardinal doctrine of the Nazi world view, Szálasi held strangely inconsistent, almost incomprehensible views on the Jewish Question. Although he described himself as an *a*-Semite not an *anti*-Semite, or someone who ignored rather than hated Jews, he envisioned Hungary as a state without Jews. He insisted on carrying out the final solution of the Jewish Question—a gradual resettlement of the Jews—with regard to the interests, mainly economic, of Hungary and the racial peculiarities of Hungarians, not by imitating the Nazi model.

However, theory is one thing, practice is another. By the time the Arrow Cross Party took power and Szálasi became the self-styled Leader of the Nation, nearly all the Jews in the countryside had been sent to concentration camps.

Szálasi's undisciplined and brutal followers viewed themselves as the last defenders of Christian traditions and the racial purity of Hungary. On October 16 the doors of all star-marked houses were sealed and the remaining supplies of food and medical aid were cut. Brutal Arrow Cross gangs started their reign of terror. Between October 16, 1944, when Szálasi became prime minister, and February 13, 1945, the day on which the Soviet troops completed the liberation of the whole of Budapest, acts of cruelty and unimaginable savagery became common, everyday occurrences. A forced march of about 60,000 Jewish men from Budapest to the Austrian border in the bitter cold of the last winter of the war so weakened and decimated them that even the Germans complained of not having received deportees in usable condition.

In the ghetto, set up in November, the daily rations were reduced to 690 calories and up to fourteen people lived in each room of every apartment. Sadistic Arrow Cross extermination squads made daily visits. They moved and acted freely. They would beat or shoot to death anyone they wished, or gather and march groups of Jews to the Danube where the icy waters of the river carried away bullet-ridden bodies.

On January 18, 1945, the Soviet forces completed the occupation of Pest. The ghetto was liberated, and its surviving inhabitants poured through its gates into a city that had been reduced to rubble. The fighting in Buda, on the other side of the Danube where the royal palace and government buildings were situated, raged on. The members of the Arrow Cross militia, following in the footsteps of the last German defenders of the "Queen of the Danube," as Budapest was called, were resolved to erect one more bloody monument to their infamous legacy. They broke into hospitals and dragged gravely ill Jewish patients out of their beds, beating or shooting them to death. Then the Arrow Cross men hunted down those who had lived in hiding or possessed false identity cards. Their fate, too, was certain death. On February 13 the Soviet forces seized Buda and the guns fell silent. The battle of Budapest had ended. Of 825,000 persons considered Jews in the 1941–45 period in greater Hungary, about 565,000 perished and about 260,000 survived the Holocaust.

Today about 80,000 Jews live in Hungary. Synagogues, the famed Rabbinical Seminary and the Jewish High School, rabbis and cantors, and charitable and cultural institutions are the constant reminders of the failure of the Nazis' Final Solution. Every Jew in Hungary is a living symbol of the indestructible will to survive and to rebuild.

The Jews of Hungary have preserved both the traditions and the creative spirit of their thousand-year-old community and the memory of their fallen relatives and coreligionists. Despite the permanent wounds of the soul, life goes on.

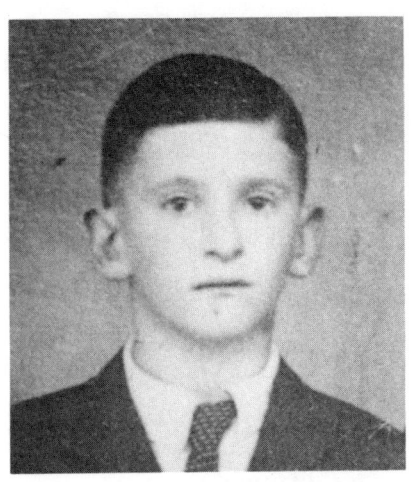

GABOR KALMAN

WE PRETEND

Kalocsa is an old, historical Hungarian city 74 miles south of Budapest. Once it had a thriving Jewish community. Out of the 12,000 inhabitants, 900 were Jewish. My family owned a lumber and building materials business. We were well-liked and respected, not only within the Jewish community but also by the mostly Catholic population in the city and the outlying farms and villages. Anti-Semitism was a fact of life, but physical violence against Jews was unknown to us.

Remembering . . .
Dressed in my blue suit and black-patent-leather-and-white-suede shoes, the mark of a well-dressed eight year old of the time (1942), I was on my way to school on Main Street in Kalocsa wearing a *kokárda* on my lapel. A *kokárda* is a

rosette made of a ribbon of red, white, and green, the Hungarian national colors. It is worn on March 15, the holiday commemorating the heroic freedom fighters of 1848 who fought for Hungary's independence. Jewish elementary schools, just like all other schools in the country, observed this holiday. Although there were no classes, a special celebration was held. As I was turning the corner, three boys slightly older than me jumped out of an alley and proceeded to beat me up. "You stinking Jew!" they shouted. "You shouldn't wear a kokárda! Go to Palestine!"

Dirtied, bloodied, and my kokárda torn off, along with part of my blue suit, I turned around and ran into the safety of our house. I asked my parents, "Where is Palestine, and why do I have to go there?"

My mother and I went to our tailor; not for a fitting of a new suit for me, but to have yellow stars made for the family. We would have to wear them when leaving the house.

The doorbell rings in the middle of the night. It keeps ringing. I am afraid in my room and go to the living room where I find my parents in silence in the dark. Someone is pounding on the front door. The doorbell does not stop ringing. My father turns on the light and opens the door. Three SS officers come into the living room. They speak politely and quietly with my parents. I don't understand German and I am sleepy, but I can sense the overwhelming concern of my parents. I look at the well-dressed, clean, polite officers uncomprehendingly. I sense danger, but don't know why. Then my eyes discover the menacing skull-and-crossbones insignia on their uniforms.

The pounding on the front door becomes a nightly routine.

We are moving to the ghetto. I am not sure I know what a ghetto is, but moving is usually fun. I am somewhat disappointed when I find out that the ghetto is my grandmother's house and a few other houses around it. My cousins and my friends are going to be there, too. It might be fun living in the same house with friends even though each family has only one room. The grown-ups do not seem to view this as fun.

My father comes home in the middle of the day and has a very agitated conversation with my mother. Then they go to their bedroom and start packing. They do not see me, but I overhear their hushed dialogue. Father was stopped on the street by an SS soldier and a Hungarian policeman. The SS soldier had a list and my father's name was on it. The policeman recognized my father and motioned toward a truck by the curbside that already had several Jewish men on it. Some of them were relatives of ours. My father rummaged through his pocket and produced a dry-cleaning bill, explaining that it was a summons for him from Budapest where he was due to depart immediately on behalf of the war effort. The SS soldier turned to the Hungarian policeman, who because he knew my father and didn't want to turn him in, verified his story. They let him go. That evening my father left for Budapest. We never saw the people on the truck again.

A few days after my father left, my Uncle Laci arrives at our house in a taxi from Budapest. A Budapest taxi in Kalocsa was an unusual occurrence. There is terror on my uncle's face as he tells my mother to pack immediately and tells me that what was to follow would not be fun. My mother packs a small suitcase, not the great black patent leather one we usually took to Budapest or Lake Balaton. Although it is late spring, she asks me to put on my overcoat. The minute we are in the taxi, my uncle makes sure that the overcoat covers up the yellow star on my jacket.

We drive into the night. Just as we reach the outskirts of Budapest, there is a roadblock. SS and Hungarian soldiers are stopping all vehicles and checking papers. I notice that my uncle's face turns white. At that moment, the sirens start to wail, signaling an air raid. In the confusion I hear my uncle's voice: "Keep driving until we get to my brother's apartment in Budapest!" he shouts to the cab driver. "If you stop, you are dead! I have a gun!"

When we arrive at my Uncle Imre's house, my father is waiting for us. My aunt and my grandmother had arrived a few days earlier. To this day, I don't know if Uncle Laci really had a gun or if he was bluffing.

We pretend to be a Christian family, refugees from Transylvania. We stay in an elegant pension (hotel) in Budapest. There are even barons and counts there. The Jews in the city are rounded up in daily raids. We barely dare to go outside. Soon it turns out that some of the counts and barons are Jews with fake identification papers. The place is not safe. We are all at the mercy of the concierge (doorkeeper), who tries to turn away the SS every time they come to check identification papers. When she fails, the SS round up the men and order them into the toilet to see if they are circumcised.

On October 15, 1944, the Arrow Cross takes over the government. We flee the pension with only the clothes on our backs. Uncle Imre obtained some protection papers for us. As a lawyer, he still has some connections in high places. On our way to his apartment, my mother and I are accosted by an Arrow Cross militiaman. He is no more than fifteen years old. He blocks our path as if playing cat and mouse. The false papers in our pockets cannot hide the terror on our faces. Still, he lets us go.

My father is now a notary public and my uncle is a priest. They are forging new Christian documents for me, so if the family perishes at least I'll survive. We already have Swedish, Swiss, and Vatican protection papers, but one never knows which will work. As I take a furtive look out the window, I see Jews rounded up in the neighborhood by the Arrow Cross.

As soon as I acquire my brand-new identity, I am taken away by a strange man whose sister once worked for the family. I see my father counting a lot of money and handing it over to the man, along with my overnight case. It barely occurs to me that I may never see my parents again. I overhear that they'll have to report to the racetrack, where all Jews will be issued "new identification papers" the next morning.

The man who took me home brags to the neighbors that he may be a Fascist, but he is no fool. He is hiding a Jewish boy, just in case Hitler will not win the war. I call my uncle and tell him that I don't feel safe there. Uncle Laci picks me up and takes me to a private school run by one of the orders of Catholic priests. The next day he picks me up, and tells me that he found out that most of the boys there were Jewish. It was too dangerous for me to stay there. A few days later, the Nazis discover the school and take away all the boys.

My Uncle Imre's ex-secretary takes me for a walk to get some fresh air. She is a ravishing beauty and I feel safe in her company. As we walk by the Danube we catch a glimpse of a firing squad executing Jews. They fall into the icy river.

The owner of a brick factory from whom my father used to buy materials for his business has hired him as a brickmaker. My father does not look particularly Jewish and is in great physical shape, so the workers accept him for what his forged papers say he is. My mother obtained some medical papers exempting her from reporting to the authorities. Indeed, her heart is weak and she can barely stand the repeated separations of the family. She is hiding out in my uncle's apartment.

I am taken to the palatial home of a former high official of the pre-Fascist Hungarian government. The man is an old friend of my Uncle Imre. I feel safe for a few days, until the man's son-in-law shows up wearing the armband of the Arrow Cross. Uncle Laci takes me back to Uncle Imre's apartment. My aunt shows up about the same time. She was also in hiding outside Budapest, but someone recognized her on the street. She narrowly escaped.

It is my tenth birthday. There are no birthday cake, guests, or gifts, but there are real fireworks outside and we hear heavy gunfire in the distance. It is snowing. Air raids are more frequent, but we are afraid to go down to the shelter. On Christmas Eve, an artillery shell hits the building next door. The siege of Budapest begins.

There are about eighty people living in the cellar, which has turned into an improvised air-raid shelter. There is no heat or electricity. Water and food are very scarce. We moved down, risking discovery. All the windows in the apartment on the fourth floor are shuttered. The constant shelling and bombing made it impossible for us to live there. The superintendent knows that we are Jews. He knew the family before the war and doesn't report us to the frequently visiting SS and Arrow Cross.

I have a job. I make candles from wax or melted-down candle drippings. In exchange I get some food. We melt snow for drinking water, and I try to trap some city pigeons for dinner. When I finally succeed, I release the poor bird, for it is skinnier than we are. Our neighbors find a dead horse and happily return with frozen meat.

I have lice.

In a rare break in the bombing and shelling, we venture out to the quiet, snow-covered streets. The city is quiet—no streetcars, the buildings are in ruins. We throw a few snowballs. I stumble and fall, tripping on something. It is a frozen corpse. I take a close look. I don't know him. I never saw a corpse before.

Uncle Laci appears with a loaf of bread.

Gunfire is no longer heard coming from the distance. There is fighting in the streets. I am afraid to go to the bathroom. The superintendent lets me use the empty coal bin.

One morning the superintendent's wife appears. She is teary-eyed. "They took my blessed candles and they are here," she says. And they came: two tattered, tired Russian soldiers. It was somehow anticlimactic, but for us, the war was over.

A few weeks later, to escape the scarcity of food and fuel, my parents and I made our way back to our home in Kalocsa. Hitchhiking on trucks and freight trains, it took us several days. It is a leisurely two-hour drive from Budapest today.

We arrived on the day of the weekly market. Food was certainly more abundant in the countryside. The peasants who saw us couldn't believe their eyes. Among the merchandise displayed at the marketplace, I spotted a batch of children's dresses made from a very familiar black-and-white material. It was the material of which *tallits* (Jewish prayer shawls) are made.

We finally reached our house. Two Russian soldiers, armed with machine guns, stood guard at the gate. Our home had been turned into a stable. The house was totally empty. Horses were quartered on the parquet floors. We glanced into the garden where our forlorn piano stood. It served as a hitching post for the horses.

When we tried to explain who we were, the soldiers turned us away.

But we were alive. We survived the war.

Most of my relatives and friends were taken from Kalocsa to concentration camps and killed. The few survivors scattered over the world. Today there are no Jews living in Kalocsa.

Gabor Kalman graduated from the Jewish High School of Budapest in 1953. His university studies were interrupted by the Revolution of 1956, during which he left Hungary and settled in California. He is an award-winning documentary filmmaker. He teaches film production at the Art Center College of Design in Pasadena and at USC School of Cinema-Television in Los Angeles.

PETER O. MILCH

I AM NOT GOING!

March 1, 1944, was a special day. It was my uncle's fiftieth birthday, and the entire family turned out to celebrate. Relatives from all sides and friends from all over town gathered at my uncle's house for a big birthday party. My aunt, a good cook under any circumstances, really outdid herself. The finest cold meats, salads, and patés were arranged on the large dining room table amid flowers and other decorations. It was the first time I tasted caviar, and I was also allowed to have some champagne. I was almost nine years old.

Eighteen days later it was my aunt's birthday but there was no party. That was the day German troops occupied Hungary, and nobody was in the mood to celebrate. We did go over to my aunt's to wish her happy birthday, but the conversation was rather subdued. Everybody knew what the presence of the Nazis meant for the future of Jews. More than once that night I heard doubts being expressed about future birthday parties and celebrations.

The Germans did not waste much time. They decided that our two-family house on a quiet street on the outskirts of Budapest was the ideal place for a Gestapo headquarters. The fact that the house belonged to Jews made the decision much easier for them. First, they just came to inspect the house for its suitability. Four or five officers walked in, ignored our presence completely, and methodically went through the whole house, quietly talking among themselves. I am not sure I understood all the implications of this "visit." Nevertheless I was somewhat frightened. I am saying "somewhat frightened" because there was another feeling also. I had always been fascinated by uniforms. To me, the most beautiful thing in the world was a picture of my father from the First World War. He was sitting on his horse in full-dress uniform, complete with riding boots and ceremonial sword, with a crane feather in his cap. Small wonder that I felt honored to be in the presence of the highly polished cavalry boots, the shiny belts and medals, and the colorful ribbons on the neatly pressed tunics of the German officers.

The officers left without saying a word, but their faces showed satisfaction. A few weeks later the Germans were back at our house, this time just one or two officers and a half-dozen enlisted men. They shouted *"Juden herauss!"* and gave us fifteen minutes to pack and get out. This time, there was no fascination with uniforms, no beauty to admire, just pure fright and for the first time, anger.

For my parents, this eviction was not totally unexpected. They had prepared for it since the first "visit," and now that it had materialized, we simply took our suitcases and walked over to my uncle's. Once there, I quickly realized that no matter how bad a situation was, there was something good in it. Living at my uncle's gave me a chance to spend much more time with my cousin Paul. Paul was—and still is—a year older than I and in addition to being my cousin, has always been my best friend. School was out and we were together all day, playing our usual games. We played war. Paul was an American general, I was his British counterpart. Together we beat the hell out of the German army and were going after Hitler. We planned some good things for him. Just around this time, air raids were becoming more frequent. They came mainly at night, which gave Paul and me even more time to play our games.

The air raids did not really scare me. Getting up in the middle of the night and going to the shelter was more of a social event for me than anything else. At the shelter I could meet some of the kids from school, and just being up in the middle of the night made me feel more grown up.

These "fun days" did not last long. Soon we had to leave my uncle's house and move into one that was specifically designated for Jews. Paul and his family did not have to move with us because my uncle was a doctor, and, as such, he was exempt from this rule. But not for long.

In the meantime, my father was taken away to a labor camp. Fortunately, he was stationed not too far from Budapest and could, on rare occasions, come back for a short visit. Naturally, he was always accompanied by a military guard. Generally, these guards were, at least on the surface, friendly people. They would help whenever they could, knowing that they would get a generous tip.

One day, when my father came for a short visit, he brought a big, two-pound box of cordial-filled, chocolate-covered cherries. I have no idea how he got it because such delicacies had not been available in stores for a long time. He probably paid ten times the normal price because he knew how my sister and I loved them. Of course, the box of cherries became our most prized possession and we wanted it to last forever. We each had only one a day, before bedtime, and refused to brush our teeth afterward because that would have killed the taste. This went on for more than a week and we still had more than half the box left.

Then, one morning, an old lady who lived in the house

looked out the window and spotted an Arrow Cross man standing on the corner. He was in full uniform—green shirt with an Arrow Cross armband, black riding pants and boots, and a military-style cap. Looking in the other direction, she saw another man, dressed the same way, but he also carried a gun. She quietly closed the windows and ran all over the house, telling everybody that the Arrow Cross men had surrounded the entire block and were heading our way to take everybody away. The panic was instantaneous. Scared, people cried, prayed, or just sat motionless. My mother took out the backpacks that we had prepared for such an occasion. There was a change of clothing, bandages, simple medicines, and some foods that would not spoil (sardines, crackers, and candy) in our backpacks. They served as all-purpose survival kits that we had had ever since conditions became dangerous. We carried them with us when we went to the air-raid shelter and had them ready for more extended trips. The contents were never changed except to make the clothing suitable for the season. Now, we were sitting on the edge of our beds, backpacks at our feet, waiting. Suddenly, my sister and I looked at each other.

"The cherries!" we blurted out almost in unison. "No Arrow Cross bastard will eat *our* cherries," I yelled as we ran to the cupboard where the box was kept. We stuffed ourselves with the cordial-filled chocolates until we were practically green. We must have had at least a dozen each. Then, with our stomachs a bit queasy, we sat down again and waited. We sat there for a while, probably minutes that seemed like hours, but nothing happened. Somebody went to the window and peeked out from behind the curtain. The street was empty; no Arrow Cross men were in sight. The danger was over. People went back to their normal activities, but my sister and I could not move. We did not eat for the rest of the day. Still, we felt good thinking that we had done something heroic. We saved our chocolate from the hands of the enemy.

A few days later, without any warning, a couple of Arrow Cross men accompanied by some local policemen came into the building. They said that they only needed women for a few days, for some emergency work in a nearby brick factory. Nobody believed them, of course. As they walked through the house, room by room, they picked out only the younger women (those under fifty) and told them to go to the courtyard. The Arrow Cross men walked ahead and left the policemen behind to make sure that all the women gathered in the yard. This was a stroke of good luck because, generally, the policemen were less vicious than the Arrow Cross fanatics.

With only one police officer in sight my mother quickly handed him some bills. He counted them and found the amount satisfactory. After making sure that nobody saw him, he shoved my mother back into the room and quickly closed the door. All in all, they took away about twenty women. For the next several days things were pretty quiet in the house. Then, to everybody's delight and surprise, all the women came back. They were unharmed, just very tired and very hungry. They had worked in the brick factory, slept on the floor in woodsheds, and had eaten watery potato soup three times a day.

Slowly, summer came to an end. Schools opened in September, but they opened without us. Jewish children were not allowed to go to school. I would not be telling the truth if I said I missed it a lot. One day, on my way to Paul's house, curiosity got the better of me. Instead of going straight to Paul's, I took the "scenic route," going past our old house. I had not been by the house since we were kicked out by the Nazis. I just wanted to see what it looked like without us. My heart beat a little faster as I turned onto our street. I was purposely walking on the side opposite our house to have a better view.

The first thing I saw was a huge flag with a swastika flying from the top floor. Then I saw an SS guard, machine gun in hand, standing at the door. I wanted to stop for a few seconds, just to look at the windows to see if they had left the curtains in my room. All of a sudden it dawned on me: I was wearing a yellow Star of David on my jacket. The SS guard might not like the idea of a kid like me staring at the house. That machine gun in his hands looked pretty ominous. If he shoots me, my mother will kill me, I thought. I turned around as quickly as I could and went to Paul's.

Shortly after this incident came the High Holy Days. We were not allowed to go to Temple, and I really missed some of the festivities. I always loved the sound of the *shofar* (ram's horn trumpet), but there was none this year. By the time Yom Kippur (Day of Atonement, the holiest day of the Jewish religious calender) came around, I had decided that because of the special circumstances, for the first time in my life I would fast all day. My mother disagreed with me about this. She said I was too young to fast all day. After a lot of arguing and begging, she agreed to let me fast till lunchtime. I had different ideas. An hour or so before lunch, I said I was going over to Paul's and would eat there with him. Once there, I told my aunt that I had already eaten and did not want lunch. I could not bear seeing Paul have lunch, so I pretended that I had to go to the bathroom and stayed there for fifteen minutes. Around two o'clock, I went back to our house and told my mother that I had lunch. I was ready to eat the woodwork. In addition, I felt weak, dizzy, and was ready to faint. My mother, of course, noticed it and started questioning me. I gave in and admitted my scam. She gave me some soup and bread and, when the color finally returned to my face, a long lecture.

"Your intentions to fast all day were noble and understandable," she said. "However, it would have been just as effective to fast until noon. On the other hand, by disobeying me and by not telling the truth, you have ruined all the good you could have done."

The next big event came in October. The news came on the radio that Admiral Miklós Horthy, the regent of Hungary, had taken the country out of the war. He declared neutrality, which of course meant that the German troops had to leave. The joy was indescribable. My cousin Eva, who was about twenty at the time, picked me up and danced around the yard with me. For the first time in months, everybody was smiling, laughing, singing, and dancing. We were all convinced that the bad times were over and that by the next day we would all be going back to our own homes. Nothing could have been further from the truth. Within a few hours the Arrow Cross Party took over the government and declared their loyalty to Hitler.

The government was no longer satisfied with keeping the Jews isolated in designated houses scattered all over the city. Jews were ordered to move to a central location where they could be eliminated easily and quickly. Just around this time, my entire family—I have no idea how—received Swiss letters of protection. These documents were still honored at the time, so instead of moving to the ghetto, we were allowed to move to a house that was under Swiss protection.

The move itself was a frightening event. The house was far away from where we lived and we had to take several streetcars. In spite of having the Swiss letters in our pockets, we did not feel safe. We had heard of too many cases of the Germans or Hungarians simply ripping up the letters and taking the people away. All of us carried folded up newspapers which, placed strategically under an arm, would cover the yellow star we were all wearing. But even with this trick, a group of people walking with backpacks and suitcases was quite a conspicuous sight.

Making matters worse, by the time we got off the last streetcar we still had to walk a few blocks to our new home. However, by then the time period during which Jews were allowed on the street had expired. We had no choice but to start walking, hoping that we would not be caught. With the newspapers held firmly under our arms, we started walking. We were about to turn onto another street when a man walked by us and whispered: "Turn back and go around the block. The Arrow Cross men are catching your kind on this street and taking them straight to the Danube." Being taken to the Danube meant a lineup on the banks followed by machine-gun fire. In other words, certain death. We thanked the man and followed his advice. We arrived safely at our Swiss house.

When I heard the adults in the family talk about the "Swiss house," I expected something that resembled chalets I had seen in magazines. This Swiss house was quite different. It was, by Hungarian standards, a large building. Built in the shape of a square around a cement courtyard, it stood five stories high. The main entrance of the building was at one of the corners and led into a spacious lobby. Crossing the lobby, one could walk out into the courtyard through two big glass doors or, on the other side of the lobby, reach the staircase. The staircase was wide, with marble steps and a polished wood banister. The entire staircase from top to bottom was protected from the courtyard side by a glass wall. In spite of the frequent air raids the opaque glass was still in place, so from the courtyard one could not see inside the stairwell. Incidentally, there was an elevator, too, but it did not work.

On each floor there were two doors leading to an open walkway with a wrought-iron railing. These walkways ran around the entire building on the inner or courtyard side, and the individual apartments had their entrances from there. One apartment on each floor, however, had its entrance directly from the staircase. On the other side of the courtyard, opposite the main staircase, was the so-called service staircase. The stairs were simple cement steps, completely open from the courtyard side, leading from one floor to the next. In normal times, this staircase was used primarily by the superintendent of the building and the janitors when they cleaned or performed other chores. Now, it was just another staircase.

Once inside the building, we felt safe again. We were assigned to an apartment on the third floor, together with four other families. Our family was the largest. It included Paul and his parents (doctors were no longer exempt), a few other aunts, uncles, and grandparents, and us. Altogether there were sixteen of us, therefore we got the largest room in the apartment, the living room. It is hard to describe what it is like for sixteen people to sleep in one room. Five people slept on a convertible sofa bed that normally slept two. Some of the older people, like my grandmother, slept on love seats or recliners not much bigger than cribs. The rest of us slept on the floor. The families in the other rooms were as crowded as we were.

At first, I couldn't quite understand why this particular house was selected to become a Swiss house. Later, I found out that the original tenants of the building who lived there in normal times were predominantly Jewish. Out of the twenty-five or so apartments in the building, three belonged to Christian families. These families still lived in the house but did not share their apartments with others and went about their day-to-day business as if nothing had happened. There was one Christian family on the fifth floor, one on the fourth, and one on the second. Generally, they kept to themselves, but when the chips were down, they turned out to be helpful and sympathetic.

Everybody in the building knew that the Swiss protection was good as long as the German or Hungarian authorities did not want to challenge it. As a second line of defense, one of the original tenants of the building, a Jewish dentist, took matters into his own hands. He had served as a captain in the Medical Corps in World War I. He still had his old uniform, and he took it out of mothballs. Every morning, he put on his old uniform, complete with an armband emblazoned with the Royal Crown, and parked himself in the lobby. He greeted every stranger who walked in with a snappy salute and introduced himself as Captain R—, commander of the building. He was successful in turning away several Arrow Cross boys who were just looking for fun by rounding up a few Jews and taking them to the Danube. The building we lived in was separated from the Danube only by the width of the street.

Shortly after we got to the Swiss house, my father was either released or escaped from the labor camp and joined us in the cramped room. By this time it was late November or early December. It was quite cold but, of course, heating was out of the question. The front was also coming closer and closer, and one by one we lost our utilities. Electricity was the first one to go. It was replaced by candles. Then the gas went. There was a wood-burning stove in the kitchen, and some of the furniture—curio cabinets, breakfronts—really served no useful purpose. Need I say more? Finally, the water pressure was so low that we could not get any water on the third floor. First, we walked down three flights, got water from a faucet in the courtyard, and carried it up. Later on, we just had to walk up to the roof, collect some clean snow and melt it.

Throughout all this, somehow we got food, too. I really have no idea where most of it came from, but we ate a lot of beans, lentils, and potatoes. Occasionally, a brave soul, a Christian friend or business associate of my father, or a grateful patient of my uncle, risked his own life to bring us food. Those days we ate well. We had black bread, "liverwurst" made out of green peas, and other such delicacies. One night we had nothing left but two bars of butter, brought in the day before by an angel of mercy. We cut it into thin slices and ate butter.

One morning late in December, with the temperature way below the freezing point, my uncle looked out the window and spotted two dead horses in the alley behind the building. After a short conference it was decided that the horses had died of starvation and not of any disease, and that the meat must have been safe since it was "refrigerated." Some of the men sneaked out and carved up the dead horses. Unfortunately, they were so skinny that we could only use the rump. We had "beef stew" for lunch that day, and it was the best meal I had in all my life. We even ignored an air raid because we did not want to put out the fire in the stove. Most of our meals in those days were cold. Air raids were frequent, even during the day, and we were glad if we could finish cooking our meals. Eating them while hot was out of the question.

Shortly before Christmas, somebody brought in a newspaper. In it was a large advertisement: "Christmas gifts for all from Uncle Joe." We knew that Uncle Joe was a reference to Joseph Stalin and that the Russian troops were getting closer and closer. With the help of my father, who spoke Slavic languages, everybody started learning Russian phrases to greet the liberating troops.

Conditions were getting worse. We were hungry, cold, uncomfortable, and scared. But in spite of all this we managed to find some humor. One day a good Samaritan brought some fruit. It was a fruit native to Hungary and it had a thick, leathery skin. One of our elderly uncles, a denture wearer, could not handle the thick skin. He chewed several pieces for a while but gave up, placed the small, wrinkled brown skins on the edge of his plate, and walked away from the table. At this point Paul walked in. "Doesn't anybody want these raisins?" he asked, and without waiting for an answer, ate the skins my uncle spat out. Paul was not very happy when we told him the origin of those "raisins," but at least the rest of us had a good laugh.

Life went on in this fashion. We had our difficulties with food, water, cooking, and heating. We had our fears of the Germans, the air raids and Arrow Cross men. At times something amusing would happen, but generally we just sat around waiting for the war to end. There was no doubt in anybody's mind about the outcome. The only question was: Will it be in time for us?

Then, early in January, a large contingent of Arrow Cross men, led by the most feared and most hated Fascist commander, came into the building. They ignored the signs indicating Swiss protection and started rounding up the people from each apartment. As we were walking out of our apartment, the commander was standing right next to our door. He had a neatly trimmed salt-and-pepper Vandyke beard.

He wore a long, brown leather coat complete with an Arrow Cross armband, brown riding boots, and a green Tyrolean hat. In his brown-leather-gloved hand he held a long bullwhip ending in a large brass ring. I did not see him hit anybody with it, but the idea of how it must hurt made me cringe.

They did not take everybody. They picked people, apparently at random, and told them to walk down the service staircase in the rear and line up in the courtyard. The four of us—my parents, my sister, and I—were among those who were sent down. We took our backpacks and started walking. By the time we reached the courtyard, it was about half-filled with people. We stood there quietly, realizing that for the first time the situation was absolutely hopeless. After a few minutes of standing there, my father stepped out of the line and started looking around. There were no guards in the courtyard. Nobody stopped him or warned him not to look around except my mother, who kept telling him to get back in line. Suddenly, my father made a decision. "I am not going," he said in a determined voice. My mother, not sensing his determination, became sarcastic. "I did not realize they gave you a choice," she said. "Get back in line and don't try anything foolish." My father, however, could not be shaken. "We are not going," he declared again. After looking around once more he glanced at us and said, "Follow me." With that he started walking, calmly and deliberately, toward the front of the building with the rest of us behind him. My mother was still muttering about it making no difference whether we would be killed then or an hour later. Still, she came, too.

When we reached the glass doors, we simply walked into the lobby. It was empty. My father headed for the stairs and started walking up. We followed him. The main staircase was also deserted, and since the opaque glass walls were still intact, nobody could see us from the courtyard side. At the second floor we stopped. My father was noticeably out of breath and had to hold on to the banister to support himself.

"If anybody, any Arrow Cross guy, wants to know what we are doing here we'll tell him we were sent back because I am very sick. Understand?" he said, and continued walking up. We reached the third floor. My father opened the glass door slightly and peered out onto the walkway. A man was standing right near the door. He was the Christian tenant from the fourth floor. I don't think he recognized us but he had a fairly good idea of what we were trying to do.

"Shut the goddamned door!" he hissed between his clenched teeth. Then he inched toward the door and gave us further instructions in a barely audible voice. "The bastards are combing through the house for the second time. They are finished with the fifth floor and are now on the fourth. They are using the back staircase so they can keep an eye on the people below. Go up to the fifth floor, very quietly, and stay inside the stairwell. Don't go out on the walkway."

We thanked him quietly and slowly walked up to the fifth floor. The apartment that opened directly from the staircase had its door wide open. The dumb bastards apparently had not realized that it belonged to a Christian family and broke open the door when nobody answered their knocks. The family had gone to work. We walked in and closed the door. We took our shoes off so that we would not make any noise and came up with a new strategy. We put our backpacks and overcoats in a closet and got into bed.

"If they come back a third time and find us here, we'll tell them that we were left behind because we are sick," said my father. "They are too stupid to remember that the apartment was empty to begin with." He had barely finished the sentence when sirens signaled an approaching air raid. We decided it was in our best interest not to go down to the shelter.

The air raid was the closest and strongest we had ever had. The explosions were so near and so powerful that the whole house shook. At one point, a window, frame and all, blew out of the wall, flew over the bed I was in, and landed in the middle of the room. My only injury was a lot of dust in my hair and my nose. The air raid lasted about an hour. When it was quiet again and the "all clear" signal sounded, we looked out the front door of the apartment. The big glass panes separating the stairs from the courtyard were gone on every floor. The front staircase was as open as the back stairs. We saw people walking around, and we knew it was safe to leave our hiding place. About three-quarters of the people had been taken away as soon as the air raid started. The Arrow Cross men swore that they would come back for the rest but they really did not have a chance. The front moved very close and we had to stay in the shelter all the time. Air raids were followed by artillery fire day and night. In about two weeks, the Russian troops reached our part of the town, and for us, the war was over.

My father had always been a mild-mannered man. To this day, I do not understand where he got the strength to say: "I am not going."

Peter Milch graduated from St. László High School in Budapest in 1953. His studies at the National Rabbinical Seminary were interrupted by the Revolution of 1956. At that time he left Hungary and settled in the United States. He continued his education, receiving his B.S. in zoology from Columbia University in 1963, M.A. in biology from Brooklyn College in 1967, and Ph.D. in biology from New York University in 1970. He has held various research positions in hospitals, universities, and industry. Presently, he is a senior research scientist in the Department of Ecology and Evolution at SUNY at Stony Brook. Dr. Milch is married to the former Jacqueline Furman. They have three sons, Stewart, Kenneth, and Erik, and live in Coram, New York.

ÉVA SZÉKELY

BECAUSE I WANTED TO BE AN OLYMPIC CHAMPION

The geographic location of a country often determines the fate of its people. As a child I often heard that Hungary was the gateway between East and West. Whatever could have made our ancestors settle here? people would ask jokingly. Who knows if the many wars we lost wasn't the doing of our bad politicians? My life is like the life of my native land. Despite my successes and the fact that many people are envious of me, I was regularly defeated on one point. No community ever embraced me fully. Although I felt in my heart and soul I was part of my community and was enthusiastic about its ideals, it was always made known to me that I was an outsider.

From the time I was a little girl, I was big on being a Hungarian. That's the way it had to be. I was still in kindergarten when I recited "Rump Hungary is no country, whole Hungary is heaven." The *"Himnusz,"* Hungary's national anthem, has always been and will always be the most beautiful melody to me. Even after being a social outcast for so long, I am overwhelmed with emotion whenever I hear it.

In the summer of 1936, during the Berlin Olympics, we were vacationing at Csillaghegy (a resort near Budapest). The heat was tropical. At the pool the broadcast by popular sportscaster István Pluhár of the finals of the men's 100-meter freestyle blared through the air. I can still hear it, "Csík! Csík! Csík!" Then came the official announcement of the victory of the Hungarian Ferenc Csík and the crowded stands fell silent. Many thousands, filled with emotion and with tears in their eyes, were listening to the sounds of the national anthem, honoring a countryman. Then and there I made a resolution—I, too, would be an Olympic champion and bring similar honor to my unjustly dismembered country. My father was from Transylvania, my mother from Felvidék, or Upper Northern Hungary.

At home, too, the conviction in me grew that what had been ours was taken away illegally from us Hungarians. I went to a German school. Then it was one of Budapest's best schools, and I loved going there. The student body was completely international and coeducational. On the other hand, the teachers were little more than missionaries of the Third Reich. They were sent there in 1933 with the purpose of using propaganda to prove the superiority of the German race. Still, the years I spent at the school were wonderful.

Then came 1938 and Hitler. In school I found a piece of paper on which a malicious cartoon had been drawn with the caption, "Erger-Berger-Schossberger, every Jew is a scoundrel. Jews, get out!" Who could have done it? For four years I had lived in an ideal community with boys and girls who were my classmates. Although various letters next to our names on the identification papers stood for religious persuasion, we children became aware of that distinction only when it was time for the religion class. Then we split up into groups and went to different classrooms.

Who could have written it and why? Where would we go and for what purpose? Why was Hungary their country and not ours? I was restless throughout the next class. During the break the Jewish students gathered. Four boys were among them. We decided that we should seek satisfaction and take revenge. I decided on the most direct approach. I stepped in front of the class. "Who wrote that?" I asked. Tom, a freckled-faced boy, stood up, sneering. He told us that it was he. "The Jews are cowards," he declared. "They won't dare tell anyone about it."

I glanced at the Jewish boys. I saw that they were scared. Tom was right. They were cowards. I hated them more than the enemy. "Next break you come down to the courtyard," I said to Tom. "I'll show you a coward." I was ten years old.

When the bell rang the whole class rushed down to the courtyard. We started to fight and I got the first real beating of my life. I held my own for ten minutes. The supervising teacher did not interfere; he let us beat each other. We returned to the classroom looking a mess. What really hurt was not wherever I'd been hit but that I belonged nowhere. In my heart I was attracted to Tom because he stood up for his contemptible deed and was brave enough to fight for it. I certainly did not belong to my seemingly cowardly coreligionists.

I calmed down after I got home. For the first time in my life my father talked to me as if I were an adult. Perhaps I did not fully comprehend everything he wanted to tell me, but I understood one thing. The situation was only temporary. I was a Hungarian. When all the madness was over one's religion would make no difference.

Three years passed and I became a member of a new group. It was the swimming section of Ferencvárosi Torna Club, a famous sport club in Budapest. No questions were asked there. Only two things mattered: how talented one was and how earnestly one trained. Within a year I was a member of the team that won a national championship in river swimming. Two months later I was excluded from the team for being an undesirable element. That was not an easy thing for a fourteen-year-old girl. Still, I believed what my father had said about a better future when I would be accepted for good and become a full member of the community into which I had been born.

Between 1941 and 1945, in the era of inhuman horrors that engulfed me and when madness reigned in the world, there was but one option left for me. I sensed that the sole means of my survival was an obsession with realizing my childhood dream: I would have to do everything in my power to become an Olympic champion. It never occurred to me that I could die, fall ill, or never again have the opportunity to swim. I wanted to win at any cost. Every night I went to sleep hearing the rising sounds of the *Himnusz* played in my honor.

It was about 5:30 in the morning on Sunday, March 19, 1944. We were walking across Margaret Bridge on our way to practice. My friend was a blonde, blue-eyed, beautiful girl. Suddenly German soldiers sitting in open trucks came into view. Rumbling tanks followed them. No one else was walking on the bridge. The young soldiers waved to us enthusiastically. "Don't wave back," I said to my friend. "It's not proper." Yet, like all seventeen-year-old girls whom the boys noticed, I was at the same time very proud.

At the door of the swimming pool Imre Sárosi, my coach, was waiting, deathly pale. "Go home at once," he said. "The Germans have moved in. We'll see what happens. Take care of yourselves, girls." For the first time in his life he hugged us and kissed us on both cheeks. At home I noticed that my father was frightened. It seems ridiculous now, but I was the only one in the family who was not scared. Nothing worse could happen to me, I thought, than not to be allowed to compete.

I was wrong. It would take too long to list everything that

did happen. But basically, the Germans decided that we should be exterminated, and I decided to win an Olympic championship. When I could no longer bear to comply with the ban against going out into the street, I volunteered to help clear the rubble. I moved twice as many bricks as the others. I wanted to strengthen my arms. I did calisthenics in the morning and in the evening. Our relatives had been ordered to move in with us. Fourteen people now lived where only four had lived before. It was virtually impossible to move around. I adapted my calisthenic routine to a space no larger than one by one meter (about one square yard).

Coach Sárosi was taken to the front. We heard nothing more about him. After the Arrow Cross takeover I, too, was taken away. The first day I decided to escape at first chance. For that, however, I had to wait a long time. We were forced to do completely useless work. We dug tank traps at Vecsés, a town ten miles (16 Km) southeast of Budapest, ostensibly to halt the Soviet tanks. Even a well-developed cow could have jumped over our traps. One day we were ordered to march through Budapest in the direction of Budafok, an outer district. It was the chance I had been waiting for, I thought. The column came to a halt. German soldiers lined the road. Perhaps one of them would help. I approached a young soldier who looked my age.

"Please, take me back to Budapest, otherwise I'll die," I said in German. After all, I had attended their school and spoke their language as well as my own.

"Are you German?" he asked in amazement.

"My mother is," I lied without batting an eyelash. It seemed to work.

"Wait," he said. "I don't know which way we're going. Let me find out. I'm sorry, we're headed in the opposite direction." He looked at me with an expression of sincere regret.

In the evening we heard that Margaret Bridge had been blown up. "Listen," I said to my friend, "if we ever get to the other side of the Danube, I'll escape at once."

"You're crazy," she replied. "If they catch you they will kill you on the spot."

"Stay if you want," I replied. "I'm going."

We slept in a doghouse that night. We were lucky. Despite the cold November weather most of the group slept in the open. Next day the whole group set out toward Budapest. We marched in rows of eight. Guarding alternately at the end of each row were a soldier, an Arrow Cross man, and a policeman. Soon we were in Budapest. I was alert as never before in my life. My whole body waited for the right moment to spring to action. I knew if I failed it would be the end of me. We were almost out of the city. We passed by a safety island. As the space got narrow, the marching order broke up. A streetcar pulled up by us and stopped.

Now or never, I thought. The streetcar conductor rang the bell. The wheels screeched. I jumped on the last step well. No shots were fired, nobody shouted. The streetcar started moving. I felt someone's gaze. A middle-aged laborer was staring at my yellow star.

"If you turn me in they'll shoot me dead," I said simply.

"Take that star off, you poor girl," he replied.

The streetcar pulled up to another stop. The man got off. I was alone. I had no idea what I was going to do. How would I get home? Were my parents alive? If yes, where were they? I got off at the next stop. People were coming and going. Some looked me over, others passed by me. I was a pitiful sight. For five weeks we had been washing ourselves with water out of a can. My clothes were ruined. My legs were covered with bruises. An old woman caught up with me and passed me. Then she came back, looking around.

"Go to Benczur Street," she whispered. "There is a protected house there. Get on a streetcar at the next corner. That'll get you into the city. You'll find it from there. Comb your hair."

She was gone before I could reply. I found Benczur Street. I was told that I would be given identification papers the following day. Then I could start searching for my parents.

Next morning I stood in line. Suddenly I noticed my mother. She stood by the entrance. I was speechless. My God, they're alive! my brain screamed. Then our eyes met.

"Mom!"

"My little Éva!"

Later she told me that she had recognized me only by my eyes. Forty-one people lived in my parents' two-room apartment in St. Stephen Park. I became the forty-second. The house was under Swiss protection which, however, hardly gave protection. By the time we were liberated only ten of us were left. The rest had been taken away or shot and pushed into the Danube.

My sister and I spent the nights lying on top of the gas oven. As I could not fall asleep under such circumstances, I figured out how I would keep in shape. The staircase was the only empty part of the house. Five stories, twenty-six stairs to a story. God created them just for me. At dawn I climbed over eight people and started from the main floor up. Five stories up, five stories down. At first I did it twenty-five times. Soon I found the number too low so I did it fifty times. Later I raised it to seventy-five and finally settled on an even hundred. Then I sat on the floor and did calisthenics. The others were still asleep when I returned. Thus I had the unusual good fortune of being able to use the toilet and the shower without standing in line. I was contented.

One morning when I had done about thirty-nine rounds I noticed an old lady, one of the residents of the house, standing at one of the turns with a candle. She looked frightened until she recognized me.

"Éva, my dear, what are you doing here?" she inquired. "Is anyone ill?"

"I'm strengthening my legs." I replied truthfully.

The lady thought that she did not hear me well. "You're doing what, my little girl?"

"I'm strengthening my legs."

The old lady turned without a word and started walking in the direction of our apartment.

"Mr. Székely! Come at once! Something terrible happened to little Éva."

My poor father jumped off the desk that served as his bed. The commotion drew more and more people to the staircase.

"Éva, what on earth are you doing here?" my father asked. "Come on in at once. You'll catch a cold." He escorted me inside. By nightfall the whole house knew that the Székelys' younger daughter had gone mad.

I decided that it would be simpler to do my thing openly during the day. As long as they thought I was crazy I might as well go all out. From then on I walked up and down the five floors a hundred times twice a day. I even modified my routine by walking up every other floor on tiptoes.

We had hardly anything to eat. The daily ration was two spoonfuls of poppyseeds mixed with honey. The reason we chose that delicacy was that the only things we had left to eat were poppyseeds and honey. My parents begged me to stop walking the stairs. It was to no avail.

The people in the house had gotten used to it. At times other youngsters even joined in. I stopped only when the fighting reached the house and we could not leave our apartment. Then, finally, the last German soldier and the last Arrow Cross man were gone. Three days after the liberation Coach Sárosi came back. He had escaped from the front and followed virtually in the footsteps of the Soviet soldiers. When we met we stared at each other for a long time. For me the war ended at that moment. Things had worked out: I stayed alive and I was ready to swim.

Éva Székely realized her childhood dream: She won the gold medal in the 200-meter breaststroke at the 1952 Olympic Games in Helsinki and the silver in the same event four years later in Melbourne. She was the holder of numerous national, European, Olympic, and world records. She and her former husband, three-time Olympic champion water-polo player Dezső Gyarmati, are the parents of Andrea Gyarmati, winner of the silver medal in the 100-meter backstroke and the bronze in the 100-meter butterfly at the 1972 Olympic Games in Munich. Andrea is now a pediatrician. After she retired from competitive swimming, Éva Székely became an internationally respected coach and educator. The author of three best-selling books based on her experiences, she lives in Budapest.

MARTHA HENTZ

LET THOSE WHO STEAL A CHILDHOOD BE PUNISHED

I love music. I consciously choose the type of music I feel like listening to. When I was a little girl I also enjoyed beautiful, sonorous music, but at the same time an inexplicable, sad feeling filled my heart. What if anything should happen to my mother? As I was listening to some music I felt as if an ominous sign had touched me.

Many years have passed since then. It is not easy to recall the past. The feelings stir me still and they are painful.

Now, if I glance in the mirror, I see a middle-aged woman, my brown hair interspersed with gray. Two adult women call me Mother. A beautiful, one-year-old boy could call me Granny, if he could talk and did not live more than six thousand miles away.

I could not have left my parents to go so far away. But

then, in November of 1944, the Nazis took my mother far away from me, to a place from which people cannot come back. Nine years old, I learned then a never-ceasing deep sorrow. Even now, Mother's Day is the saddest day of the year for me.

A little girl leads a pleasant, sheltered life. She spends her days playing with friends. The nearby factory grounds offer an inexhaustible source of amusement. One day the children have an argument. "You are a Jew!" shouted the children. The girl stood there stunned and could not comprehend why being Jewish should cause a mocking remark. During the next few weeks such mocking shouts occurred more often in school. She also noticed that the family became more tense and troubled.

When the airplanes roared above and began bombing Budapest, people in the girl's house sought the relative safety of the factory's air-raid shelter. The girl was terrified but was comforted by the presence of her family. She felt that her mother's caressing arms could shield her from all dangers.

Life became progressively more difficult. The Nazis took her father to a forced labor camp. The house was declared a Jewish house and was marked with a yellow star. The parents' treasured little apartment became crowded with two additional families who were forced to share it. After October 15, 1944, events accelerated quickly. The few short hours of glimmering hope were followed by the deepest despair in the hearts of the adults.

On a fateful November day, the Nazis took the father away. The girl wished that she could have the strength to kill the Nazi who then took her mother and the others in the transport. She remained alone with the strangers in the apartment house. The people in the house took care of her for a few weeks until her father came back. Since he was older than the required working age, the Nazis let him go for the time being. When he found out that his wife had been deported, he wept. It was the first time the girl saw her strong, courageous father sob.

In a few days all the inhabitants of the house were commanded to move into the crowded ghetto area. This time Grandmother also moved in with them. The family loaded their sparse belongings on a cart and moved into a building on Síp Street. The little girl took along a few toys. The most important was her precious plastic doll.

The family was assigned to an empty apartment. Fourteen people lived in a medium-size room. They settled on the floor close to the walls. There was a bakery on the ground floor that radiated a little warmth through the floor along with the wonderful smell of freshly baked bread. There was no place to cook, but there was nothing to cook anyway. Fortunately the communal kitchen sent some food on most days. Beans one day, split peas the other.

During the day, if it was not extremely cold, the children walked around the fenced area of the ghetto. Corpses and dead horses lay scattered on the sidewalk. The children stepped over these without much concern.

The girl walked every day to the entrance door of the Jewish Community office. Posted on the door was a list of those who managed to come back to the ghetto from deportation transports. She hoped desperately to see her mother's name on the list. Each day brought another disappointment.

When the weather became very cold, the water pipes froze. It became more difficult to acquire water for washing. True, the children did not much mind not being able to wash themselves.

The war was nearing the end. Air raids continued almost without pause. Hundreds of bombs fell, and many hit the houses in the ghetto. Besides starvation, the air raids caused many casualties among the Jewish population. When the sirens sounded, everyone ran to the shelters, taking their sparse belongings. The girl always took her precious plastic doll.

During the last days, people could not even come up from the air-raid shelter. Day and night became the same now; only a small candle flickered in the room.

Once, during a few moments' lull in the dreadful, dull rumble of the explosions, the girl dared come up from the moldy, dusty shelter. She approached the entrance door and took a look at the quiet street. Suddenly she panicked. She felt as if the blood froze in her veins. A German soldier passed on the sidewalk, a revolver in his hand. Luckily he did not notice her.

All the ghetto dwellers were fortunate that the Germans did not have sufficient time to explode the mines they had laid down in the ghetto.

Finally, January 18, 1945, arrived. Russian soldiers in white camouflage suits, red stars on their caps, came and searched for German soldiers in the shelter. All they found were starved, pale children and women and old people hardly more than skeletons. Everyone is free, they said. The walls of the ghetto were demolished. The people were allowed to go home. Unfortunately few had homes to go to. The soliders tore off the yellow star from the girl's coat and gave her a slice of bread, a sign of their good intentions.

Father, Grandmother, and the girl left the ghetto and went home. Their house had no windows left and was uninhabitable in the bitter cold. For lack of anything better, they moved into the guard's room of the neighboring factory.

Father walked every day to his former place of work. Slowly, life returned to normal. School started to function. Spring arrived with new hopes. Everyone eagerly waited for the return of the survivors of the concentration camps. The girl waited for her mother in vain.

Time cannot be stopped. The girl began studying in the Jewish High School. She grew more mature and studied well. She found a wonderful friend whom she loved as a sister.

Finally, in the Jewish High School, she met a boy whom she would marry years later and for whom it was worth surviving to share a life with.

MARTHA HENTZ

Martha Hentz graduated from the Jewish High School of Budapest. She met Tibor Bauer there, and they were married in 1956. She has devoted her life to her husband and their two daughters. She has recently become a grandmother.

ANDREW HANDLER

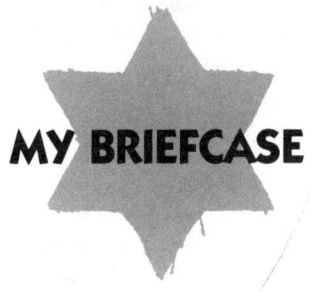

MY BRIEFCASE

It was a few months before my ninth birthday that I began to realize that there was more to life than going to school every day and playing soccer just as often. By then nearly five years had passed since the start of the war. I cannot say that I was put out on account of it. Things around me had not changed much. In fact, I had a good time just being a healthy and active boy. I had a small group of friends with whom I played soccer in a small park near a well-preserved ancient Roman amphitheater across from the apartment building where we lived. The gates of the amphitheater were always shut even though in the middle of it there was a large, grassy clearing that would have made our games so much more enjoyable. I often thought about what it would be like playing there and imagined the stands filled with cheering Roman fans.

Like everyone else, I had priorities: my parents, my brother, my friends, soccer—oh yes, and school. Actually I happened to be a rather good student. I learned fast and was often told that I had nice handwriting. The building that housed the Jewish Elementary School of Óbuda, the district of Budapest where I was born, was large but friendly looking. My teacher was a kind, patient, soft-spoken woman. Her husband was the principal of the school. She was also a friend of my mother's, a fact that did not exactly make me ill at ease at school and of which I often reminded myself when I cut short my studying so I could meet my friends in the park. I never took advantage of that friendship, however.

Óbuda had a large Jewish community then (there's but a handful of Jews now, mostly elderly) but I became aware of its true size only on my way to and from the synagogue. As my father and I walked the cobblestoned streets I saw many people, wearing their best clothes, walking in the same direction. We exchanged greetings with many of them as we did again in the synagogue, which was usually filled to capacity. The synagogue was an imposing structure with an ornate interior. It was more than a hundred years old by then and never failed to impress me. It stands deserted now. The rabbi, a silver-haired and bearded elderly man with a soft voice that could hardly be heard in the rear of the synagogue, had the reputation of being a great scholar. Still, my thoughts were often on the large fenced courtyard where I knew I could always find some of my friends. In short, I was a happy-go-lucky fellow unaffected by life's unpredictable, often distressing, turns. All but one. It had to do with the fact that the Jewish Elementary School of Óbuda, like all Jewish schools, held classes on Sunday, instead of Saturday when all non-Jewish schools were open. From Monday to Friday I was simply one of many schoolboys on their way to or from school. On Saturday, by the time we started our walk to the synagogue, most non-Jewish schoolboys had already gone to school. Sunday was different. On that day only Jewish children went to school, although their parents stayed at home and did not go to work. Thus all of the people I saw on the street were Christians, dressed in their Sunday best and on their way to church.

I have no idea what it was that started making me feel uneasy. Let it suffice that I did feel uneasy. As I passed a person or a group of people, clutching my briefcase, I felt certain that there were expressions of disapproval on their faces and unfriendly flashes in their eyes. On Sunday I was clearly an outsider in my hometown, I thought, trespassing on their day of rest and prayer. The thought that on Saturday the tables were turned crossed my mind, but I did not feel any better for it. I was annoyed for feeling the way I did but could not help it.

As time went on my discomfort grew. I decided to do something about it. I knew there was nothing about my appearance that gave an indication of my destination on Sunday. I was dressed properly—shirt, sweater, shorts, knee-high socks, and shoes—and my hair was combed. (For years I was less than pleased with my hair. Because of a cowlick it had to be parted on the right. I thought only girls parted their hair on the right but it rebelled against all my efforts to force it to part on the left.) There was one hitch, however. It was that briefcase of mine.

Here I must digress a little. As if it wasn't bad enough that my hair did not part on the left, I was stuck with a briefcase, the kind that is held by a handle or carried under one's arm if one wanted to appear casual. All of my friends had schoolbags that were smaller than mine and worn on the back with straps around the shoulders. I never understood or learned my parents' reason for buying me a briefcase. However, it turned out to be a durable companion and eventually a useful and undemanding ally.

Back to my Sunday predicament. I still don't know what made me do it, no one had ever said anything offensive to me about my being a Jew or going to school on Sunday. I had certainly never been ashamed of being a Jew as I knew virtually no non-Jews and had spent all of my nine years among my coreligionists.

Clutching my briefcase on my way to school one Sunday morning, I stepped up to an elderly couple and politely asked directions to a street that I knew was in the other direction. Surely, I reasoned, a well-dressed boy on Sunday, even if he was carrying a briefcase, would be thought of as a stranger who had lost his way to relatives or friends. As I was being directed to the street in question a feeling of relief came over me. I was no longer an offender, a trespasser. (I would only like to know what strange quirk of reasoning convinced me that by stopping someone for directions I would automatically gain the acceptance of all those who would pass by me for the rest of the way. At nine, I guess, one doesn't burden himself with rationalizing.) I waited until my benefactors were out of sight before I resumed my journey to school. After a few steps my confidence in my disguise evaporated. "You dope!" I mumbled. "The only person you managed to fool was yourself." I quickened my steps, trying to leave the scene of my short-lived triumph as fast as possible.

The second time I tested the usefulness of my briefcase was soon after the Germans occupied Hungary on March 19, 1944. I watched the long line of gray-uniformed German soldiers and rumbling trucks from our second-floor balcony. I didn't really comprehend the gravity of the situation. Uniforms had always impressed me. Among my friends I was the only one who knew all of the military ranks and insignia of the Hungarian army by heart. I also liked to watch marching soldiers, listening to the sounds the nail-studded soles of their boots made on contact with the cobblestoned streets. I liked the sound so much so that once, to the great consternation of my parents, I pushed dozens of thumbtacks into the soles of my shoes and walked up and down the linoleum-covered foyer of our apartment. The sounds the thumbtacks made were very much like those of the marching soldiers.

My infatuation with the military received a terrible boost by a visit I unwittingly paid to a most unlikely place. We had a maid, Margit, a young Christian peasant girl. She spoiled me badly so we got along famously. In return I did not tell my parents about the times she would entertain soldiers in her room after my parents had gone out in the evening. Once Margit took me to a meeting of the local Hitler Youth organization. I recall seeing flags with the swastika in the middle and many boys who wore black shorts and khaki shirts with black ties. Clearly I was impressed. I don't remember if I told my parents about my visit or asked them if I could have a uniform like the ones I had seen. All I know is that one day soon after my visit to the Hitler Youth, Margit was gone. I didn't get the uniform either.

Soon thereafter my mother sewed a piece of yellow cloth, shaped like a six-pointed star, on my overcoat. I felt that I'd be wearing it for a long time because my mother sewed it on with tight, small loops. "All Jews must wear it," she explained. I didn't have to wait until Sunday to feel like an offender. The moment I stepped across the threshold of our apartment I knew I was a marked man. There were no ifs, ands, or buts about the bright yellow Star of David. Instinctively I raised my briefcase, covering the star, as if to shield myself from all the passersby to whom my identity would be all too obvious.

This attempt to disguise myself was even shorter lived than the first one. "Who am I kidding?" I thought. A briefcase held in an unnatural position would only make everybody curious about why I was doing it and what I was concealing. With a sigh of resignation I lowered the briefcase. I walked through the large door of our apartment building and into the street, clutching the briefcase by the handle so firmly that my knuckles were turning white.

It didn't take me long to get used to wearing the yellow star. Much to my surprise, nobody paid the slightest attention to me or what I was wearing. The yellow star became a part of my coat, and I went around as unperturbed as before.

My world of illusions, however, was soon shattered. One day my only Christian friend, a boy somewhat older than I, offered me a ride on his bicycle. "I want to tell you something," he said. I jumped on the crossbar. As we circled the small park near our apartment building, he started speaking in a low voice. "I'm very, very sorry about all this," he said. "I've heard that you and your people will soon be taken away and killed."

I didn't really understand what he was saying. Of course I knew about the war. I was aware of the large number of armed soldiers in Budapest, and I was told that some of our relatives living in the countryside had been taken from their homes. Often in the middle of the night the sirens started wailing, and we had to run down into the basement that served as an air-raid shelter. But I wasn't aware of anybody who was actually killed. Why should I, why should we, be killed? My friend did not know and said nothing more about it.

Even though my aforementioned priorities left me little time to think about the war, I could see that with the Germans in town things had changed already. Some of my friends were nowhere to be seen. Even though it was nearly the end of the school year nobody spoke about vacation, let alone about being in a higher grade in the new school year. My friend's warning kept haunting me. I couldn't get it out of my mind. I spoke to no one about it. It would be my secret, I thought.

A few weeks after that my father was ordered to report to a forced labor camp and my mother told me that we would leave our home. She packed a few necessities and readied my baby brother for our departure. She explained to me that we would go to a safe place, assume different names—mine would be Pista—and have to say "Christian" if anyone asked about our religion. When we walked by an empty field, she tore off the yellow stars from her coat and mine and threw them into the bushes. With that we became outlaws and fugitives. As we walked on, my friend's warning came to my mind again. Only then did I realize that when someone was forced to leave his home, he would need something bigger than a briefcase to protect him.

I learned about the details of our escape years later. My father, who had been a director in his brother's textile factory, bought the identification papers of a Christian worker's wife and two sons. After he left for the labor camp my mother wrote a letter. In it she announced her intention to commit suicide. By the time the letter was found she would have done it. She had given her two sons, she wrote, to a "Christ-fearing" couple for safekeeping. She placed the letter on the table in the living room. Then the three of us disappeared. Her plan worked. Nobody looked for us.

Our destination was a small house in one of the outer districts of Budapest. The owner of the house, a well-meaning person who lived there with his wife and elderly mother, had an expensive and frustrating hobby: betting on horses. The promise of a great deal of money in exchange for room and board for the three of us apparently increased both his compassion and betting spirit. To be sure, he was playing a deadly game. If our presence in his house was discovered, he and his family could be shot.

By the time we arrived at the house, a few other Jews were already there for the same reason. When we left a month later, the number of those who had sought refuge there had risen to twenty. Conditions were, to say the least, undesirable. The amenities designed to accommodate a couple of people now had to provide for over twenty. We often stayed in the cellar and were allowed to go out into the garden for a breath of fresh air in small groups only at night. Some vacation, I thought.

We did not stay in the small house long. The constant fear and tension made the tight quarters feel unbearable. As my mother's anguish grew and her patience wore thin, it was decided that the three of us would leave the house and try to slip out of Budapest. Our destination was Hajdúszoboszló, a spa famous for its thermal baths, in the eastern part of Hungary. Our host's wife volunteered to accompany us. I was given extensive instructions. I understood that the success of the operation would largely depend on my ability to assume the identity of the Christian boy I was supposed to have become. I would be told many times later that I played the role to perfection.

On the train we had a hair-raising experience. We happened to be sharing a compartment with a couple of gendarmes, notorious for their brutal treatment of Jews. When it was time for my brother's diapers to be changed my mother stood up, preparing to take my brother to the lavatory. The gendarmes, however, wouldn't hear of it. My mother should change the diapers there, they said, insisting that they would not be inconvenienced. They even offered to help.

Acceptance of this unexpected gesture of cooperation would have been disastrous. In those years only Jewish male children were circumcised. The thought of my brother lying naked in front of the two gendarmes prompted my mother to act quickly and decisively. She grabbed my brother and the two of them left the compartment amid words of "thanks but no thanks."

In Hajdúszoboszló we settled into a life of utter boredom, occasionally interrupted by moments of fear. Not only did I have to play the role of a Christian boy I also had to look and sound like a peasant boy. My head was shaven, and I received clothes that I wished I would never see even in a nightmare. Within weeks I also learned many words and expressions native to that region of Hungary. The way I sounded when I spoke left no doubt as to my being a born peasant. (When, after the war, we returned to Budapest and I was enrolled in the Boys' High School of the Jewish Community of Budapest, my classmates would often look at one another upon hearing me speak as if I was some strange, alien creature. It took a few months for me to get rid of that embarrassing legacy of the war.)

My life in Hajdúszoboszló was a far cry from the sad and tragic experiences of my friends. The war came there by way of an accident. The town had no strategic value. In fact, a the rumor went around that the reason it was spared the ravages of war was because the mother of the King of England regularly received shipments of bottled water from the town's famous mineral wells. I don't know if there was any truth to the story, but it sounded believable. Only one wayward bomb fell on the town. It did no damage but killed the mayor, the only person in town who, I was told, had made some outlandish comments about Jews.

It was also during my stay in Hajdúszoboszló that a situation similar to the one I had been in with regard to my briefcase developed. In rural areas all males wore knee-high boots. All but me. For some reason I did not get boots, which made me feel just about as frustrated as my briefcase had months before. Then in September 1944, the Russians occupied Hajdúszoboszló. Before they arrived the townspeople were taken in by rumors of a ravaging horde of Asiatic barbarians. We were relieved when we discovered a couple of bearded Russian Jewish officers who showed great kindness to us upon learning our true identity. They even gave me a pair of the boots I had been wanting since our arrival in Hajdúszoboszló. However, one boot was black, the other brown. I couldn't have cared less. We were free.

A few weeks later another event of almost miraculous nature took place. In the wake of the Russian forces many of the liberated forced laborers started returning. Among a group of them passing through Debrecen, one of the largest cities of Hungary, was my father. There he learned of our whereabouts and within days we were together again.

With the liberation my days of merely watching the local school from a distance came to an end. My parents arranged to have the principal of the school give me private lessons that enabled me to continue my studies without the loss of time. He was a nice enough man and did not make me work hard. Although he probably had nothing to do with it I would spend the next eight years chasing good grades that for me were all too elusive. Even my once nice handwriting deteriorated to a barely legible scribble. Often I blamed my mounting misfortunes on him.

We only heard about the atrocities of the Arrow Cross and the suffering of our relatives and friends in Budapest. It seemed unbelievable that we should be liberated before their hours of final reckoning began. Fortune smiles at some people even in times of tragedy.

It was in late spring of 1945 when we returned to Budapest. Amid the ruins there were signs of new life. We went back to our apartment in Óbuda. It stood empty. Our neighbors, thinking that we had perished, had helped themselves freely to everything we had. I took a quick look around the room that had been mine. We left quietly, closing the door of the apartment for the last time. Suddenly the picture of the briefcase, probably the most memorable possession of my childhood, flashed through my mind. I made it disappear as quickly as it came. It was a memento of a past I preferred not to remember.

Andrew Handler graduated from the Jewish High School of Budapest in 1953. His studies at the Rabbinical Seminary of Hungary were interrupted by the Revolution of 1956, during which he left his native country and came with his parents and brother to the United States. He received his B.A. from the University of California, Berkeley, in 1959 and Ph.D. from Columbia University in 1967. He is a professor of history at the University of Miami and lives with his wife, Deborah, and his mother in Coral Gables, Florida.

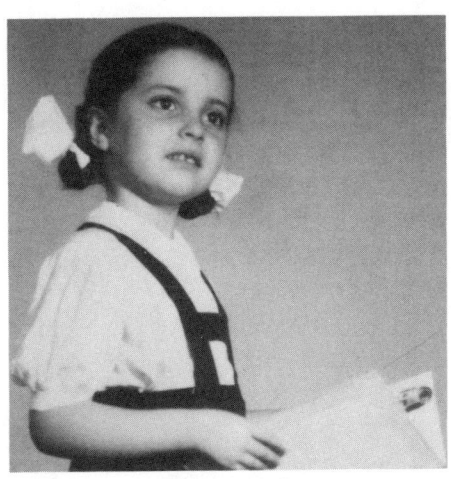

SUSAN V. MESCHEL

THE BEGINNING OF THE END

Caesar was my first playmate. Actually he was my grandmother's dog. She was the only person he obeyed and listened to. Caesar was a large, shaggy, honey-brown dog with soulful brown eyes, floppy ears, and a somewhat hesitant, uneven gait. He took his duties as watchdog very seriously. My paternal grandparents had a tiny house with a huge garden at the foothills of Buda. The house had a flat roof, where we liked to play with the pebbles, sunbathe, and talk. Caesar joined us, but even there, if he saw anyone pass near the fence he barked with a fierce intensity. Caesar hated motorcyclists and German uniforms. At the sound of a motorbike or the sight of a soldier he would work himself into a frenzy and chase them as far as he could. Caesar also took it on himself to patrol the garden. This was a difficult job, for my grandparents owned many fruit trees, and during the summer the ripening peaches, apricots, and plums provided temptation to hikers.

My favorite spot was a large cherry tree in the upper portion of the garden. It was easy to climb and wonderful to perch on the lower branches, munching on cherries and reading stories. Caesar usually sat below, waiting for me to climb down and play with him. My grandmother let her grandchildren roam freely about the large garden. She always said, "They will come home when they get hungry." The same applied to Caesar.

Another of Caesar's duties was to watch that the hens, roosters, and ducks did not go over the fence into the neighbor's garden. The chicken coop had a wire fence my grandfather put up, but one or another overactive rooster or goose occasionally poked a hole in it and got out. When that happened, Caesar heroically chased them back to the coop. Once a duck crawled under the fence into the neighbor's yard. That particular neighbor owned a beehive. While chasing the duck, Caesar got too near the beehive and came back like a wounded soldier covered with many stings. He stood by patiently till my grandmother smeared some homemade remedy over his nose and mouth.

The last Seder, or Passover service, that our family celebrated before the German occupation was attended by some twenty-five to thirty people, all members of our family. It was a warm, noisy Seder with lots of laughter and singing. For a few hours the adults tried to forget about the war and anti-Semitism; the children, including myself, were blissfully unaware of the problems of the world. For me this was a specially memorable Seder, for my cousin Erwin was there. Erwin was a slim, energetic boy with large brown eyes. He was incredibly athletic and mischievous. I, like an adoring disciple, followed him into every adventure. Erwin also had a lovely boy-alto voice and taught me many Hungarian folksongs as well as the anti-Semitic ditties of that time.

On the Eve of Passover my grandmother customarily

placed a large wooden washtub filled with water at the door. The water contained a few drops of beet juice to symbolize the Red Sea. All the grandchildren had to jump over the tub to indicate that we had personally crossed the Red Sea and therefore identified with our ancestors. At that memorable Seder, Erwin decided to jump the length of the tub and fell in. I thought it was hilarious, even Caesar had a wide grin on his face. He lapped up the spilled water.

Grandfather insisted on having only white wine at Seder. He said the goyim, or non-Jews, could misunderstand it if we had red wine. I understood only decades later what he meant. For centuries Jews were accused of using the blood of Christians for baking the matzoh for Passover. Having white wine must have been regarded as a precaution against these accusations.

Caesar's real weakness was food. He loved my grandmother's cooking. As a matter of fact, he did not care for dog food at all. He much preferred stuffed peppers, watermelon, chocolate, and matzoh balls. One Sunday my grandmother was preparing for a family gathering and cooked a large pot of stuffed peppers. The pot was cooling on the stone floor of the veranda. Caesar sniffed it and the temptation overwhelmed him. He ate most of the contents of the pot. Grandmother became rather angry, for we expected about thirty people that afternoon. Caesar lay down in front of her, looking very guilty. At first she spanked him twice on the rump, then made him camomile tea—the standard remedy at their house for tummy ache. The gathering took place anyway under the great sprawling walnut tree in the upper garden.

Caesar was part of the family. When I gathered raspberries for the annual jam-making, Caesar came along and managed to get burrs in his fur and thorns on his face. It took hours to pick the burrs and yank the thorns out. He patiently stood by, wagging his tail as if he knew that we were trying to do our best to help him.

My grandmother was a short, plump woman with beautiful brown eyes. She must have been very pretty as a young girl, judging from the photos. We loved to play with some of her old dresses, including the bustles. She read a great deal and could tell lovely stories. Saturday afternoon when everyone else took a nap, she would tell the grandchildren marvelous stories, mostly about great rabbis, miracles, or heroic deeds of the biblical kings. Grandmother represented warmth and wisdom in the large, chaotic family. It was difficult for her to bend down, so at every Sabbath it became my task to lace up her shiny black shoes. By this time she had arranged her wig, straightened the black silky dress, and put on her heavy gold chain and cameo pin. Usually Grandfather was impatiently waiting to go to the synagogue. He was a short, wiry man with a dapper little moustache. His jokes and voracious appetite were well known in the family. Every Sabbath, Caesar insisted on accompanying my grandparents to the synagogue. He walked with them to the door and obeyed only Grandmother when she commanded, "Go home Caesar, watch the house!"

In my grandparents' home there was always a lot of singing. Grandfather was a cantor and my two uncles also served as cantors. Caesar tolerated only low voices. Any time my Uncle Kálmán, who had a lovely tenor voice, hit a high note, Caesar howled.

After the German forces occupied Hungary on March 19, 1944, life changed too drastically even for small children as little aware of anti-Semitism as I was. The subsequent air raids did not make much impression on my grandparents. Their tiny house had no air-raid shelter. Anyway, my grandmother always believed that whatever fate brought, it was as "God wills it." Just to be on the pragmatic side, Grandfather dug a large hole in the chicken coop and buried all the silverware and jewelry the family possessed. Caesar and I stood by as he buried the Seder plate, the Kiddush cup, the candlesticks, and Grandmother's gold chain and pin, which had been in the family for generations.

The last to be hidden was a tiny canvas bag containing

the family's oldest piece of jewelry. This was a little gold ring with a turquoise forget-me-not stone. The ring was given as a present to Great-Great-Grandfather Nehemya. Nehemya Berger was a patriotic Hungarian besides being a devoted Jew. He enthusiastically supported the cause of the Hungarian Revolution in 1848 against the Habsburg rule. After the revolution failed, he helped hide some of the fleeing revolutionary soldiers. One, whose life he saved, gave him the ring. In the course of the counter-revolutionary reprisals, he was executed for his life-saving deed. Grandmother told us the story many times. To me that little ring always meant our roots in the country.

We all helped bring rags from the old wooden shack to cover up our family treasures. Caesar sniffed around as if trying to remember the place. Grandfather said that he hoped when the war was over someone in the family would perhaps come back and reclaim the family heirlooms.

In May 1944 the deportations began. My aunt Lenke and my three cousins were deported to Auschwitz. My father and my uncles were all on forced labor duty by this time. Once in a great while one or another was able to visit for a day or two, usually by bribing the Nazi guards with cigarettes or gold.

When my father came for a brief furlough from his forced labor unit, he continued to work in the garden as if it were peacetime. There, sunburned, surrounded by his gardening tools, he could briefly forget about the war and the forced labor for the Hungarian fascists. He took special care in pruning the almond trees.

Another hobby, which apparently took his mind off the ever-increasing dangers, was repairing shoes. On Sunday morning he spread out the tools on the terrace and with great relish hammered away and mended all the shoes in need of repair. My father was considered the head of the family, the brightest, most capable man, and in spite of the war and persecution he still tried to take care of everyone's needs. There was a serious food shortage, but with his usual foraging skills, he managed to acquire some Swiss cheese, Grandmother's favorite snack. Grandmother attempted to hold onto tradition in spite of the war by baking her Sabbath coffeecake. If I close my eyes I can still smell the marvelous aroma of that chocolate coffeecake. Caesar and I stood in the kitchen door, both of us sniffing like puppies. A slice of that coffeecake was the topic of many wistful dreams during the following time of starvation.

My Uncle Miklós's labor unit was mobilized during the summer to be transferred to the Russian front. He considered this ominous news and decided not to wait for heavenly help. In the army kitchen where he served as a cook, he poured a pot of boiling water over his arm. Uncle Miklós spent the next few weeks in an army hospital with second-degree burns. The labor unit left for the Russian front and no one survived. Uncle Miklós was one of the few men in the family who survived the war.

At the end of the summer a new law came into effect. Jews could not own pets. Grandfather tried to give Caesar to several Christian neighbors, but he always came home. Each time he ran panting up the garden path and settled by Grandmother's chair on the terrace. Eventually all the large dogs owned by the Jews had to be turned in at army stations for military duty. Grandfather took Caesar there twice, but each time he escaped and returned home. The third time we did not see him for two days. Then, a day later, Grandfather went to the market to buy some fish. He came back unusually upset for his jovial, ever-cheerful personality. His little black moustache twitched and he kept wiping his eyes. "The Arrow Cross men are selling veal and rabbit meat to German soldiers," he said. "So what," I asked, more sassy than I meant it. His voice shook and his eyes were full of tears. "Don't ask me anymore. I recognized Caesar's remains."

On April 3, 1944, the Allies began large-scale bombing of Budapest. I enjoyed the air raids immensely. There was to me an adventurous, almost camping atmosphere there, and it never occurred to me that my family or I could be killed or injured. When my father came for a brief furlough from the labor camp at Nagykáta, he promised that I could get an air raid for my birthday. As usual, I believed every word he said. He was right as on so many other times. I still remember the violent shaking of the house and the faces of the petrified people in the air-raid cellar. However, I was too busy to be truly frightened. I was learning songs from an "older" girl, almost thirteen—about twice my age—who escaped with her mother from the Warsaw ghetto. I felt tremendously flattered that such a "mature," heroic person even talked to me. Singing with Renee made me completely oblivious to the surrounding danger. I recall three of the songs: a lullaby in Hebrew, the song of the Vilna ghetto ("Never tell that this is the end of the road"), and the anthem of the Japanese Navy. A rather strange program.

On the day Szálasi and his Arrow Cross party took over the government (October 15, 1944), all the adult women were taken away from our apartment building. The house, 11 Miksa Street, was marked with a yellow star, designated for Jews only. The men had been taken away to labor camps long before. Now only frightened children remained ranging in age from three weeks old to thirteen years old.

On the second floor lived a Nazi-sympathizer couple who were in charge of "discipline." They offered to feed us moldy cabbage. I declined the offer, reasoning that the "cobwebs" could not be healthy because my grandmother never fed me that sort of food. After two days of starving, a stranger in a dirty brown uniform came to take me away—he said to meet my mother. I grabbed my favorite plastic doll and went with him. He took me to 14 St. Stephen Park, a house "protected" by the Swiss government—at least all the people who lived there had Swiss protection papers. Unbelievably, my mother was really there. Apparently, all the women from our house were taken to the old brick factory in Óbuda, which served as a gathering place for deportation. My mother bribed one of the guards with a gold cigarette case to allow her to escape. The same guard was willing to bring me to her later on for a further bribe of jewelry. All the adults in the 14 St. Stephen Park apartment hugged me and wept, for I was the first child from the house to be reunited with at least part of the family.

In the Swiss house at 14 St. Stephen Park on the shore of the Danube river, about sixty people were crammed into a lovely, modern three-room apartment. The owners must have been wealthy Jews before the war because the Persian rugs were exquisite. The bathroom had a sunken tub and even a bidet. Most of us had never seen such a luxurious place. Some of us washed our feet in the bidet and felt as if we participated in some decadent rite. Eight of us slept in a bed. Some people slept on the piano and some in the bathtub. The apartment was located on the seventh floor. The stairway as well as the apartment had lots of glass doors and windows, which gradually all broke during the constant shelling and bombing.

My father came once more to see us. He bribed a labor camp guard with 1,000 Symphonia cigarettes to bring him to us. He seemed very worn and pale, and his face had lines and folds I had never seen before. He had a little moustache, which felt prickly when he kissed me. He managed to bring us great treasures of food—a long piece of salami and some *inasz* (goose fat bacon). While the guard was out of the room my father asked my mother if she thought he ought to escape. My mother was afraid to reply. When he left, his last words were addressed to me, "Take care of your mother." I never saw him again.

A few days later some Arrow Cross men came to take a transport of people away. These people were either shot on the shore of the Danube river or deported somewhere. As we were gathering our few belongings, one of the Arrow Cross men, probably an officer, became interested in my plastic doll and indicated with a commanding lift of the finger that he wanted it. He grabbed it and pulled. I looked at the man and absorbed every detail. He wore black pants, a silver tiebar, high leather boots with large silver spurs. His little Hitler moustache twitched. He raised his machine gun and pointed it at me. I can still feel the coldness of the gun metal touching my side. Suddenly a furious, wild, defiant feeling came over me. That doll was a present from my father. He brought it from Italy when I was two years old. I felt that defending that doll was defending my father, my love for him. Intermixed was a burst of anger and some kind of rebelliousness against all that had happened. I held onto the doll with all my strength and pulled it back. We struggled for the doll for several minutes—or so it seemed. My mother stood motionless, pale, petrified. It was painfully quiet in the crowded room. I heard a loud click of a gun. Then the officer suddenly gave up the struggle and led a group out of the apartment. We were left behind and safe for the time being.

In the morning we waited for the bombing by the Allied planes. These air raids were quite punctual, usually around ten o'clock. After climbing back to the seventh floor and checking for damage, the daily guessing game began. Will the Arrow Cross militiamen come to take a transport away? By this time we knew that the Swiss letters of protection offered no help whatever. Moreover, even the smaller kids knew that the people in the transports were either going to be shot or deported.

One day a group of Arrow Cross men came wearing their traditional garb of green shirts and high boots. They commanded some fifty people to gather their belongings and be ready for transport. A feeling of the usual doom set in. We all knew what this meant. This time my mother and I were in the transport. Then one of the uniformed men read a list of names and indicated that these people should stand aside. Our names were read, among others. The leader, a tall, dark-haired man, announced that our group was signed up in 1939 to emigrate to Palestine and therefore was under the jurisdiction of some international protective agency. Suddenly, I recognized the voice of the leader. He was, in fact, my Hebrew teacher in first grade, Fabian Hershkovits. I opened my mouth to cry out his name. He noticed it and signaled me to keep quiet. Fortunately, I understood and managed to produce a blank expression. Our group of eight remained in the house. We were temporarily saved. None of us realized at the time that this was the work of the Zionist underground.

The afternoons were spent foraging for scraps of food, soaking the revoltingly colored split peas to make them slightly edible, and preparing for the afternoon air raid. The Russian planes usually came during mid-afternoon. For some reason there was more noise and fire associated with the Russian bombing than with the morning raids.

We were constantly hungry, always hunting for some food or at least for something to chew. I remember chewing a small, leathery piece of rancid bacon for more than a month. My mother found a sack of moldy, dry bread and by lengthy soaking and grinding made some round objects she called meatballs. To me these tasted wonderful. By this time only twenty to thirty people remained in the apartment from the original sixty.

To pass the time between air raids and transport selection, the remaining children on the seventh floor developed a new game which quickly became the favorite. The leader posed a rhetorical question, "What are you going to do with Hitler after the war is over?" The reply had to be creative and as complicated as possible. The best idea of the day was rewarded by one lick of prune jam. The jar was nearly empty, only a little jam was left. This precious jar was hidden inside the piano. I vividly recall my feeling of triumph, when, on Christmas day of 1944, the children voted my idea to be the best for the day. My prizewinning suggestion was that we should inject spinach under Hitler's skin. The idea had to be accompanied by highly elaborate technical details and as gruesome descriptions as possible. Immediately after the kids voted that I should get the coveted lick of the prune jam, we heard the afternoon bombing alert and ran to the air-raid shelter. I was very restless. It still did not occur to me that we could possibly die, but I was very much concerned that the apartment might get bombed and I would be cheated out of the hard-earned lick of the jam. I sneaked out and ran upstairs. The entire house was shaking violently, bullets were whistling, and broken glass fragments flew all around. My heart was beating wildly as I entered the apartment. There was a large hole in the living room wall and a large fragment of a shell on one of the beds. I quickly lifted the top of the piano, took out the precious jar, and, with a mixture of some guilt and some devil-may-care abandon, took *two* licks of the jam!

The last week under Nazi rule was full of mysterious rumors. Most of the surviving inhabitants knew that 14 St. Stephen Park had been mined, ready to be blown to smithereens before the Red Army had a chance to move in. Facing the bank of the Danube River, the house stood in the line of fire. All the windows had been broken and the stairway scattered with fragments of shrapnel, shells, and bullets.

Even during the days of destruction and tension a strange and surprisingly cheerful sight could be observed nearly every day. An attractive teen-aged girl kept running up and down the staircase with an incredible display of energy. I admired her determination to stay in good physical shape. When people dreamed only of bare physical survival, she dared to think and plan for the future. No one imagined that the purposeful, energetic girl would become an Olympic champion swimmer in a few short years.

Even in the last days, Arrow Cross men continued to take groups of Jews from the various "protected" houses to the shore of the Danube to be killed. We heard the shots and the cries. One day, a wounded boy of about eleven crawled to the door of our house and asked in a matter-of-fact manner to be admitted. We were in the air-raid shelter when he was brought in—a skinny little boy with brown, curly hair and lots of dried blood on his shoulder.

After this event the entire area became very quiet. It was a tense, menacing sort of quiet. We dared not move from the air-raid shelter. Suddenly, after what seemed like days, three Russian soldiers appeared. They had wild eyes, Mongolian faces, feet wrapped in rags, and pointed their machine guns at us. One said, *"Nemecki kaput"* (the Germans are destroyed) and made a slashing gesture at his throat. The second said, *"Tsassy,"* indicating that he wanted to be given watches.

We were finally liberated! But how different it was from the joyous, emotional experience we had dreamed about amidst fear, death, hunger, and despair. It was January 18, 1945.

The small, pitiful group of survivors had intense discussions as to what to do next with their lives. No one knew what was going on in the city after having been locked in the Swiss house for months. My mother, along with four others, ventured out of the house a few meters and sliced some meat off a dead horse. The group cooked some sort of stew that tasted slightly sweet. This was our first feast as free people. Our discussions weighed the advantages of staying in the house, which offered relative safety, or going out to attempt to find our homes and relatives. My mother and grandmother could not agree and asked me to decide. This was a tricky problem for a girl of eight. However, my decision was instantly made. "Let's go," I said. My feet were frozen and I could not take my shoes off. My greatest desire was to go somewhere where I could take off my shoes and maybe even take a bath.

We finally left 14 St. Stephen Park. The tortuous walk began. My mother was pulling a small bundle. Finally we reached a relative's house at 15 Király Street, which was in the area of the liberated ghetto. We rang the doorbell. Our luck still held out. The Mandels had survived and let us in. I do not recall much about the few days we spent with them. I liked wise, old Mrs. Mandel the best.

Nearly every day Russian soldiers knocked on our door looking for watches and adult women. Each time my mother and Aunt Aranka hid in the pantry behind the large pickle barrels, their faces blackened with coal. The blackening was supposed to be an effective deterrent to the soldiers' attention. Even though I was still a little girl they smeared my face, too. Of course I had no idea what they were concerned about. In my eyes the entire hiding process was immensely entertaining. My real problem was lice. The remedy against lice was complete shaving of the head and I was jealously guarding my long braids. While at the Mandels, we found out that my hasty, impulsive decision to leave 14 St. Stephen Park was very fortunate indeed. A former neighbor visited us and in passing mentioned that a shell fragment had hit our bed. Had we stayed there, my mother and I would have perished.

One morning the doorbell rang. At the door stood my uncle Andy, the first man in the family who returned from the Nazi labor camps. A short, stocky fellow with thick glasses, he seemed to me more beautiful than the greatest painting. Andy was alive! His very presence gave us hope that maybe some others survived, too. Then I noticed the second miracle. He held in his arms a large pot of steaming, hot *cholent* (baked beans). The smell was enough to intoxicate a hundred starving survivors like us. Andy had escaped from a forced march toward Poland. He had managed to elude capture by the Nazis and was liberated by the Red Army. They treated him rather well. He could have stayed with them in relative comfort, but he insisted on searching for the remnants of the family.

Andy accompanied us to another apartment at 13 Népszinház Street, a dilapidated house even in better times, with a movie theater on the ground floor. Our new home was a tiny, ugly, one-room apartment with all the windowpanes missing. A wretched little stove valiantly tried to keep us from freezing. My Aunt Jolan was there with her children, Judit and Eva. Judit had scurvy, her little legs were all bent. Eva was only eight months old, she could not even sit up. By this time, my Grandpa, who had owned Caesar, had joined us. He was ill with dysentery. A neighbor, Dr. Marcus, told us that Grandpa might die unless he could have some decent food and advised us to feed him mashed potatoes. That was a suggestion akin to prescribing ground diamonds for dinner. No one had such luxuries as potatoes in January 1945.

In this situation of concentrated misery Andy took command. He made arrangements for Aunt Jolan to go to a town in the countryside where she might get some milk for the children. Grandpa's case was harder to tackle. At this time there was still intense fighting between the Nazis and the Red Army. It was especially dangerous to be out on the streets. Still, Andy agreed to accompany two of his female friends across the Danube to forage for potatoes. The women knew of a farmer who would sell potatoes in exchange for some goods. They needed Andy for protection. What Andy could do against Russian soldiers was questionable. However, his reward for chaperoning them was a share of the potatoes.

The bridges across the river had been blown up by the Nazis weeks before in an attempt to stop the advance of the Russian troops. Andy and his friends had to jump over floating ice slabs to cross the river. Andy was a practical, fun-loving fellow, but certainly not the hero type. Somehow, they managed to get across the Danube and found the potatoes. The following day they returned across the raging Danube, hopping over floating, melting slabs of ice, carrying sacks of precious potatoes. That evening we roasted some on the little coal stove. What luxury!

Once Grandpa was feeling better he described in great detail the horrors of life in the ghetto and Grandma's death. Grandmother, the storehouse of wisdom and backbone of the family, had died of hunger and pneumonia. Her sole complaint was that after raising eight children she was fated to die alone. There was no way in the ghetto to bury the dead. All the bodies were heaped in the courtyard of the ritual bath.

My mother bartered her engagement ring for a small sack of flour. It was a square-cut emerald ring that my father had bought in the time my elders called peace. This was a concept of which I knew nothing. It seemed like a dreamlike state of utopia where people had food, warm rooms, and even candy.

A few short weeks after the liberation I contracted scarlet fever. This caused the family lots of problems, for there was no medication, heating, or even windows to stop the icy blast of the February wind. Mother found a doctor, who told her that we had to have a warm room, otherwise I might simply die or at least develop complications. Andy set out with great determination to improve our lot. He came back an hour later, hunched over under the weight of a huge carved oak door. Apparently, he had stolen the side door of a bombed synagogue. That door probably saved my life, for it kept our stove going for weeks. Through the haze of fever, I vaguely remember that our second family survivor returned at this time. It was Uncle Kálmán. He brought back a baby bottle full of goose fat and a kilo of sour candy. These were incredible treasures, and I still recall the taste of that wonderful Rumanian sour candy.

In my half-delirious state I listened to Kálmán's tale of survival. He had spent the last six months of the war in a forced labor camp, working in copper mines in Bor, in eastern Yugoslavia. Many of his companions died of starvation, disease, and brutal killings. At some point the Nazis set up two groups, supposedly to go back to Hungary. Everyone wanted to be in the first transport to go home. People tried to bribe the Nazis to be allowed in that group. Kálmán had nothing left to give, so he remained in the second transport. The entire first transport was killed and buried in a mass grave at Crvenka. Aunt Jolan's husband, István, and the great modern Hungarian poet Radnóti were in that group. Kálmán was liberated by the Red Army and spent a few weeks in Transylvania to recover with surviving Jewish families. Kálmán was a good cantor with a lovely tenor voice, so he was usually very welcome in the local communities.

By the time I recovered from the scarlet fever and was able to get around, it was early spring. We were still waiting for family survivors with less and less hope and more desperation. I could not believe that my father could possibly have been killed.

School began in a rather haphazard way. The classes were held in a damaged old Jewish elementary school. Some children were rebellious, cocky like myself, ready to fight at the smallest provocation. Others were teary and depressed. It was the unwritten rule among my peers to make friends primarily with children who had only one parent or none at all. I must say we were not an easy second or third grade class to handle. I vividly recall that we raced fruitworms on our desks during class. This game involved many elaborate rules for the route of the worms and the appropriate timing procedures.

Besides displaying unruly behavior we became more and more politically oriented. Some families converted to Christianity, leaving their Jewishness behind as a bad experience. Some became fervently religious, perhaps to thank God for their survival. I became a member of a Socialist-Zionist club (Hanoar Ha-Zioni), mainly because my mother allowed me to join only the organization that my cousin also attended. The Zionist movement provided us with some faith in the future, pride in ourselves, and pleasant companionship.

During these weeks a few more survivors trickled home, among others Uncle Béla. He did not talk about his experiences. There was less and less hope every day that my father would come home.

One Sunday during the summer of 1945 we gathered in the old house in Buda, so forlorn now without Grandmother to give it spirit. Grandpa triumphantly located our silverware and jewelry that he had buried in the chicken coop in 1944. We sat around the crumbling terrace watching the starry sky. A strange feeling of anticipation came over us. Grandpa exclaimed, "Someone will come home today!" My heart raced, Please God, let it be Father! Suddenly a skinny, dark, gypsylike man appeared in the doorway. We held our breaths. Who could he be? Is he a stranger asking for food? He rang the doorbell. We stared at him, a bony, skinny, sunburned fellow, his face full of bristles. Grandpa cried out. "Thank God, it is Moshe!" We hardly recognized him. He used to be a wide-cheeked, husky man with a twinkle in his eyes. Moshe was my aunt Lenke's husband from the small village of Gyöngyöspata. His wife and three children were killed in Auschwitz. A sturdy, resourceful fellow, he survived the hell of several forced marches and concentration camps, including the infamous Mauthausen and Gunskirchen.

Moshe's stories were examples of human resourcefulness and they made me deeply respect him. For example, once he climbed over the electric barbed wires of the camp to forage for food in a German village. Instead of trying to get away and save himself, he climbed back, risking his life again, to help keep a nephew and some friends alive with the food. Somewhere he found an abandoned sewing machine and traded it to the Nazis for food. I respected and loved him for defying the Nazis even in small ways. Our bond lasted a lifetime, for he married my mother a few years later.

By late spring and early summer, apartments were being renovated. People were picking up the pieces of their lives. New families were being formed. By some miraculous means we had survived—now we had to go on living. What would happen to us? The fateful year 1944–45 changed our lives beyond comprehension. Could we ever recover this lost year of our childhood? Could we still grow up into decent Jewish adults? Could we still have a future in Hungary despite what happened? God spared us, I am certain, for a special purpose. We have a cause, a purpose in this life: to grow up, have families, and tell the next generation what happened, so it never happens again.

Susan Meschel graduated from the Jewish High School of Budapest in 1954 and attended the Technical University, where she studied chemical engineering. When the Revolution of 1956 was crushed by Soviet forces, she and her family fled to Austria. In 1957 they came to the United States and settled in Chicago. After working in a cosmetic laboratory for ten months, she started graduate studies in chemistry at the University of Chicago. She received her M.S. in

1959 and Ph.D. in 1961. She is married to Dr. George Meschel, a clinical psychologist, whom she met when both were students at the Jewish High School of Budapest. They have two daughters, Judith and Eva. Currently Dr. Susan Meschel is a research chemist at the James Franck Institute at the University of Chicago.

PETER BARTA

THE BRICKYARD

The end of October 1944 found us at the second stage of our wandering since we were forced to leave our apartment in June. First, we moved to a designated "yellow star" building in Aladár Street, where the three of us—my mother, my sister, and I—had one small room to live in. On October 17, after the Arrow Cross coup, we were moved to a villa on Pauler Street, also in Buda, where some thirty of us were camping in one big room. It was about November 1 when this arrangement, too, came to an end. It was the last clear and sunny day of the autumn.

As before, we had to get out of the house on a few minutes' notice. We could only take the barest necessities, but I remember that my sister Marika, who was six years old at the time (I was ten), had taken her blue-eyed "sleeping" doll along. Our escort consisted of about a dozen guys, fifteen to twenty years old. They wore the buff coveralls of the Levente, a fascist youth movement. They were armed with one-shot Levente rifles and small Hungarian hand grenades with red and black stripes on them. These grenades looked like toys compared with the long-stemmed, professional-style German ones. The commander had a strong build and sported sideburns, perhaps trying to look older. "This commander is barely eighteen," Mother whispered. The guys all wore Arrow Cross armbands and soft, German-style caps. Not very long before, their fathers probably slapped them if they didn't eat their spinach, didn't do their homework, or smoked a cigarette. Now they had the power of life or death over us.

They started marching us down Krisztina Ring, which, despite its name, is basically a straight avenue roughly following the line of the Danube. The leaves on the trees along the avenue were turning brown and yellow. We were walking in the roadway, normally reserved for vehicles. On the sidewalk, people were talking, shopping, going about their business, enjoying the sunshine. Nobody seemed to notice a troop of old men, women, and small kids marching under armed escort down the middle of the street. It's as if we had some kind of disease too awful to look at.

We were walking south, past the steep rocks of Gellért Hill. Soon we found ourselves in home territory, our own neighborhood, the Eleventh District. Here was Miklós Horthy Avenue, the way we used to go to school, to the synagogue, to the movies, to the swimming pool—just like normal people, just a few months ago. Now we were passing through here as prisoners, destination unknown. We walked past Orlay Street, where we used to live. Here were Mr. Benkő's fruit and vegetable store—Mother used to buy the season's first cherries and strawberries from him. Weiner's bakery, Nagykovácsy's department store, Deisinger's and Meinl's, always smelling of freshly ground coffee, Zeidl's delicatessen, smelling of sauerkraut, pickled herring, and salami, Gárdonyi's bronze statue, covered with bird droppings, still stood in a minipark. The yellow streetcars—No. 9, a single car; the 19 and the 49, pulling trailers—were rumbling and clattering past us, just as they always used to. I knew them all intimately; some of them by their serial numbers, some by the advertising boards they carried: François champagne, Kollerich's wire fences.

Just past Horthy Circle, we stopped briefly at a block of apartment buildings between Miklós Horthy and Prince St. Imre avenues. We knew that the building we were standing at had two entrances, one on each avenue. Mother quickly worked out an escape plan. She was going to ask the guards to let us, my sister and me, into the building, then we were to ask the superintendent to let us use the washroom. After that, we were to get out on the other side of the building, remove or cover our yellow stars, and make our way to Rákóczi Avenue on the Pest side of the river. There we were supposed to find Éva the Swede, Mother's friend, who would hide us. Éva was a Swedish citizen who helped us get a *Schutzpass*, a document signed by the Swedish ambassador, stating that we were under Swedish protection until our departure for Sweden, which was supposed to happen sometime soon. A photocopy of the Schutzpass was sewn into the lining of my dark blue overcoat.

It was a nice plan, but when we came out of the washroom, we found two Arrow Cross guards, with rifles at the ready, right in front of the door. They took us straight back into the line. Soon we reached Fadrusz Street, where Dr. Tónay's office was. We used to see him once in a while to have our lungs checked because tuberculosis was a problem in Hungary. I wondered if he would see us now when Christian doctors no longer treated Jews. Next was the tennis club, where ladies and gentlemen in white outfits used to play, including József Asbóth, the national champion. Right by the tennis club was Bottomless Lake, reflecting the image of the two-spired baroque church on the other side, flanked by the

Cistercian High School. Behind that was the south slope of Gellért Hill, dotted with gardens and pretty villas. In the winter, we used to go tobogganing there.

Marika wandered a couple of feet away from the line. One of our guards, a younger Levente, pointed his rifle at her. "Get back in line, or I shoot," he said. Mother looked at one of the more intelligent-looking guards and said, "Aren't you ashamed of yourselves, pointing a weapon at a six-year-old kid?" She could have gotten herself killed, but instead, a conversation developed. It turned out that the guard she was speaking to had attended the same teacher's college as she did, in the city of Eger.

It was past lunchtime and we hadn't eaten all day. We turned into Bocskay Street, where the synagogue of our community stood. We had actually called it a Temple. It was a modern, flat-topped, cream-colored building that would have fit nicely into a Tel Aviv street. It had five tall, stained glass windows, a small front lawn, and a small backyard. The basement was home to our scout team, commanded by the rabbi. In '43, our school building was requisitioned by the army, and the school had to move to the synagogue. The last classes of Károly Baracs Israelite Elementary School were held here, in April 1944. The synagogue was right next to the neighborhood police station and the fire hall. For the High Holy Days services, we used to have policemen and firemen stationed at the entrances. Stones and other things had been thrown at us now and then.

When we arrived in front of the synagogue, unshaven, ragged, and tired-looking men came out to inspect us. It turned out that they were *Muszosok*, that is, Jewish labor servicemen attached to the Hungarian Army. They were unarmed, wearing bits of Hungarian uniform along with civilian clothing. They were forced to do dangerous work, such as mine removal in the front lines, from which most of them, including my father, did not return. At the time, the Muszosok were quartered in the synagogue. There had been some commotion among them; some had tears in their eyes. They must have been thinking of their own wives and children, who may have been herded along some other street. Some of them went inside the synagogue, then returned with thick slices of fresh bread and hot knockwurst. We thought we were dreaming. The knockwurst may have been made of horse meat, but it was the best knockwurst we had ever had. They must have given us their rations for the day.

Apparently there were no clear orders about what to do with us next, so we were moved to a kindergarten a few blocks from the synagogue, on Dávid Ferenc Street. We were sent into a large room with blinds covering the windows. The only exit to the street was by way of a smaller room where the guards stayed. A little later, a bleeding man covered with bruises was pushed in. He had tried to escape. Sometime in the afternoon, we heard a rifle shot from the outer room. We thought someone from our group had been executed. Actually, it was only a rifle, gone off by accident. A guard opened the door: "Did we scare you Jew bastards?" He acted as if he thought the incident was funny. Since there was no furniture, we sat on the floor. A fat, middle-aged man sat below one of the windows. He could have been a doctor, because he had a medical bag. He rolled up his sleeve, tied a rubber hose around his arm, then took a huge syringe out of his bag and injected himself. I found the spectacle horrifying. Once I had run away from school because we were about to be vaccinated and I was terrified of the needle. We speculated that the man was a drug addict, or perhaps he had tried to kill himself. Then again, he could have been a diabetic.

Night fell and everybody stretched out on the floor, trying to sleep. The guards checked on us every now and then. Sometime during the night, a small package was dropped on us. It contained a piece of salt bacon.

The next day was overcast. There was a drizzle and a cold wind was blowing—November weather. We were lined up and started marching south, along Fehérvári Avenue. This is a straight, wide road that took us past our old kindergarten, the Reformed Church with its plain, pink steeple, and the university sports club where Mother had been teaching me ice skating. The southwest line of the green suburban trains followed the road and we passed underneath the trestle of the railroad going to Vienna. Past the trestle, we entered a bleak industrial zone, with factories and great empty lots. We marched for several hours. Long walks didn't bother me: we used to go hiking in the Buda hills practically every Sunday.

We were going to Albertfalva, an industrial suburb. We got there late in the afternoon. It was almost dusk. We were herded into a construction site with some unfinished two-and three-storied buildings. The area was fenced off with barbed wire. We entered through a gate guarded by an old Hungarian soldier with a drooping moustache, his bayonet fixed, wearing a shabby greatcoat. The Arrow Cross escort didn't follow us inside. Between the buildings, there was a sea of mud. Raindrops made ripples in the puddles. We were told that we could go inside a building until further orders. The buildings had roofs, but the doors and the windows had not been put in. Wind blew through the rooms. Dirty straw had been spread on the concrete floor. Some of the women, including Mother, went outside and started building makeshift fireplaces from loose bricks. They were making "tea" from a substitute made of dried weeds. I can't remember how they got the pots and the matches. Apart from the red brick of the buildings, everything was gray and brown.

Aunt Lujza, Mother's sister, was among the women. She was running a high fever, and her face was shades of green, white, and purple. She lay down on the straw, and we kept fetching her glasses of mock tea, which smelled and tasted of smoke. There was no lighting in the building, so when it turned dark, we went to sleep. I began to lose track of the last time I had slept in a bed or taken a bath.

By the next day, we could hear distant thunder from across the river. It was cannon fire. The Red Army was advancing toward the southern outskirts of Pest, the eastern part of the capital. The front was moving toward us. It had rained steadily since we had arrived in Albertfalva. There was confusion in the camp about who was in charge and what was going to happen next. Soldiers came and went, and the general idea seemed to be to move us out of Budapest and farther behind the German lines. The Russian advance south of the city probably had ruled out taking us in that direction.

It was Friday evening, our second day in Albertfalva. A new group of Arrow Cross arrived and lined up everybody in a column, except the very old, the sick, and the children. The column was marched off on foot to Óbuda, in the north end of the city, a three- or four-hour walk. Mother had to go with them.

We were left with Aunt Lujza, who was still very sick. There was a lot of screaming and pushing. We were ordered to get into the back of an open truck. Those who couldn't climb into it were thrown and shoved. When Marika was lifted into the truck, she dropped her doll into the mud. An Arrow Cross man picked it up and handed it to her.

By now it was dark. The truck roared at top speed back north, the way we had come. The city was blacked out. There was practically no other traffic. Everything seemed dead. I took a last look at Orlay Street. I couldn't see much, just the dark outline of the nearest buildings. I had a feeling that we might never see our street again.

The truck rumbled past Castle Hill and continued north, following the line of the Danube. Finally, it made a right turn through a gate into a large, almost totally dark space. Despite the darkness, I could sense that the place was full of people. The truck stopped. We were in the Óbuda Brickyard. Bricks had been made here since Roman times.

Someone opened the tailgate. I was hit on the head with a billy club and pushed off the truck. I fell into a muddy pit. I didn't know where Marika or my aunt was. All I could see was darkness. Up until then, I thought that the Hungarian government wanted to make life miserable for us but wasn't actually planning to kill us. Governments are not supposed to kill their own citizens. I had always been taught that we were Hungarians, and the police and the army were there to protect us. Now I began to have doubts. This, I thought, must be the gateway to hell.

After a while, I managed to crawl out of the pit. I found Marika and Aunt Lujza. We somehow made our way into a shed, used for drying the bricks before putting them into the kiln. It had a roof supported on columns, but no sides. The wind was blowing through it. We sat down on a stack of wet bricks and huddled together for warmth. Aunt Lujza was in bad shape. Her teeth were chattering from the fever. It must have been about midnight. We tried to sleep. It was still raining.

In the morning, we realized that the place was enormous. There were thousands of people milling about in the mud. They must have been picked up by the Arrow Cross throughout the city. There were also all kinds of armed guards: Arrow Cross "party servicemen" who looked like criminals—some wearing party uniforms, some in civilian clothes. Then there were Hungarian soldiers, the feared gendarmes, and some Germans. A huge column was being formed. People were whispering. The column was going on foot to Austria or Germany. All hope was lost of being liberated in Budapest when the Russians took the city. The people already lined up in the column looked miserable and desperate. They must have sensed that this was the end. They started throwing their belongings away—blankets, backpacks, even food. Someone handed me an aluminum mess pot, like the one we used to carry on our hikes. There were some sugar cubes in it. We, too, were ordered to join the line.

Far away from us, at a building where the commanders must have been staying, there was a small group of civilians wearing dark hats and overcoats. There was some kind of commotion developing around them. People around us started talking excitedly. Word was getting around that anyone who could prove that he or she was under Portuguese protection should get out of the line and see the man from the Portuguese legation. Soon, this was repeated for everyone under Spanish, papal, Swiss, or Swedish protection.

At that moment, I remembered the photocopy of the Swedish paper in the lining of my overcoat. I took it out and approached the nearest uniform. As it happened, it was a grayish-green one. As far as I knew, that would have been either a German soldier or a Hungarian customs officer. I held out the paper to him. The picture on it showed Mother, Marika, and me, sort of huddled together. It was not very clear. The man could have simply torn it up, but instead, he sent us to join another, much shorter line. After a long wait, we were told to start walking toward the main gate. We were, of course, still under armed escort.

Suddenly, there was a miracle. Another column was being marched past us, in the opposite direction, presumably meant to join the big one that was going to Austria. Mother was in it. We saw each other. We held up the Swedish pass and waved her to join us. In the general confusion, nobody noticed that there were four of us using a pass made out for three.

Mother told us that she and others from Albertfalva were herded into an underground kiln for the night. The kiln had been nice and warm, presumably retaining some heat from the last time it was fired. However, they were under a wooden trap door with gaps in it, and in addition to the rain, some Arrow Cross men had peed on them.

Soon our Swedish column was taken to a ferry station on the bank of the Danube. For some reason, they didn't want us to use nearby Margaret Bridge, so we boarded a small motorboat for the crossing. The weather was still rainy and foggy. I kept busy trying to read the name of another ferryboat crossing the river to the north of us. The paint must have been worn, for it didn't make sense: POLYSAC. It took some time to figure out that it really was IPOLYSAG, the name of a region in northern Hungary. I sensed that for the time being, we were out of danger.

The next thing I remember was that we were on the Pest side, in No. 4 Pozsonyi Avenue. The district was relatively newly built, just opposite Margaret Island. It was a well-to-do, upper middle class area, resembling parts of Manhattan.

Our building was about six stories high and had a document attached to the main gate: "This building is under the protection of the Royal Swedish Embassy," in Hungarian and in German. It also had the Swedish triple crown and the seal of the ambassador on it. The building was packed with people, so they took us to the boiler room. I have never liked a boiler room as much as this one. It was warm, dry, and brightly lit. We had lawn chairs to sit in. Huge pipes, painted bright red, blue, and white, ran along the walls and under the ceiling. We were given some hot tea and something to eat.

Later on, a room was found for us, on the second or third floor. Aunt Lujza had recovered. We were sleeping in real beds and were eating decent food. We were even given a Swedish newspaper. It was the first time I saw a really big newspaper, like the ones in America. I saw my first comic strips. I remember Donald Duck, whose Swedish name was Kalle Anka. I learned a few Swedish words, based on similarity with English and German: airplane, tank, attack, German, weather, births, deaths. The Stockholm stores were advertising *oranges* for Christmas. Someday, I thought, we may actually get to live in Sweden.

One of the civilians at the brickyard that Saturday morning could have been, and quite probably was, the legendary Raoul Wallenberg.

Of Peter Barta's immediate family, only he and his sister survived the war in Budapest. They subsequently lived in Miskolc, an industrial city in northern Hungary. He completed his studies at the Ferenc Földes High School in 1958. Thereafter he studied electrical engineering at the Technical University in Budapest. He left Hungary during the Revolution of 1956 and emigrated to Canada the following year. A graduate of the University of Toronto, he is a registered professional engineer in the province of Ontario. He and his wife, Anikó, live in Toronto, Canada.

TIBOR BAUER

HAVE YOU EVER MADE A WHISTLE OF AN APRICOT PIT?

Look! That's how you do it. Come and sit down by me on the curb and rub the pit against it. You've got to do it a long time until the shell wears out and the core becomes visible. Then you do the other side of the pit. When you've got that far, it's easy to finish. With a pin you patiently remove the core bit by bit until only the pit with the two holes is left. Then you hold it to your teeth and it will whistle when you suck in and blow out air through the holes. I could play more interesting games but the older children won't let me because I'm only nine. So, mostly I lean against the wall of the synagogue and only watch the older boys play tipcat in the courtyard.

We live at 3 Pásti Street, across from the synagogue. Yes, in that one-story house with the narrow door. In our town,

Debrecen, most houses are like that. Only on wide Piac Street will you find large, multistory houses.

This, here, is our kitchen, and that is a dark passage through which we reach the room. The room, as you can see, is dark even in daylight even though it has a large window facing the courtyard and a tiny window up there facing the beer factory. The furniture consists of four beds, a table and chairs, and two commodes. It suits us—Dad, Mom, and the five of us, brothers and sisters—fine.

My dad is a hard-working and very religious man. I walk with him to the synagogue at dawn not only on *Shabbes* but every day. I'll tell you a secret. The only reason I do it is because it feels good—for him.

My father owns a small tinman's shop on Széchenyi Street where he hammers tin plates on a large iron roller so hard that the whole street rings with that sound. Nowadays, he has taken to hammering in the kitchen in the evening, which makes our neighbor very nervous and cantankerous. Dad has a good reason for doing it: He has to work hard to provide for us, and he must come home from the shop before dark. For every day after dark, young thugs armed with brass knuckles, iron pipes, and other stuff come around and beat up everyone they suspect of being a Jew. However, this troubling situation is about to end, for tomorrow my dad will be taken away and become a forced labor serviceman. Where and for how long nobody knows.

My sister Margit, who is a big girl (she's twenty, I think), says that we don't learn much anymore. The only reason we go to school is to keep busy. She also says that our lives are in danger because the Germans are here. We should ask the principal, Mr. Steiner. He is a quiet, kind, respectable man who always wears nice clothes. True, he creaks when he walks but that's because of his wooden leg. Yesterday during the first hour he talked about Jewish history. When he finished I wished he had said more. He said that the Almighty had chosen the Jewish people for Himself. I feel that if He did so—for if the principal said that He had it must be true—

then there is no reason to fear the terrible things about which the adults keep whispering

It's a little unnerving to meet German soldiers on the street. They're always so well-dressed in their olive uniforms and shiny black boots. My friend Steimetz tells me that if I stick out my arm they will salute back. Mom says I should not do crazy things like that and should get as far out of their way as I can. Dad was taken away because the Germans wanted it. The Hungarians aren't any better, either. They should fry in their own fat. I have no idea why my mother says things like that. Neither do my sisters.

What do you say to that neat looking, thick high wall with which the whole of Pásti Street has been closed off? There are, of course, a large gate and a small one, but I've never seen them open. Outside the gates, they say, stands a *csendőr*, a gendarme, who has cock feathers in his cap and his bayonet drawn.

Nothing is happening nowadays. No school, no *cheder* (Hebrew school). We can play in the courtyard of the synagogue the whole day. Only one thing is bad: for lunch, always thick brown soup. "Soon you won't have even that, my son," my mother says. I'm relieved.

We've been told that we'd soon take a trip. We still don't know where, when, and how we're going. And we won't even need to buy tickets to the train. The *nyilasok* (Arrow Cross men) will take care of everything.

The adults are already preparing to leave. Everybody is allowed to take five kilos of personal belongings. Listen, I'm going to tell you something but you mustn't tell a soul. I've noticed that Mom and my sister Rozi—you know, the one who's seventeen and already smokes in secret—buried the Singer sewing machine and perhaps even some winter clothes, judging by the length of time they were fiddling around down there. I suspected they were up to something because it had been announced that nobody was allowed to hide anything, which caused the adults to think that if they were taken away, the belongings they left behind would be stolen.

It bothers me that we have to stand in line for so long in the middle of our street. The *csendőrök* (gendarmes) are shouting and my sisters run back to our apartment to get something. At long last we start out in rows of six down the middle of the street. I didn't realize how many we were. Doesn't that star bother you? I certainly don't like that. I certainly don't like the large yellow star we have to wear on our jackets. I never cared even for medals on the lapel.

The gate of the ghetto, made of the wood of freshly chopped trees, opens. As we pass through it they count us. We turn into Hatvan Street and then left in the direction of the small train station. We keep moving in the middle of the street, keeping the rows in a straight line. We aren't going to get lost, that's for sure. Gendarmes, with guns on their shoulders and bayonets drawn, walk beside us on both sides. Many people watch us from their windows. They look indifferent. For some reason I feel ashamed.

We've finally arrived in the brick factory. The strong, grown men and the older boys are missing. They were taken away into the forced labor service. After much waiting we're assigned places under one of the drying sheds. There's a row of these long, wooden, tile-roofed structures, standing one after the other. No sides, no front, no back. Only a roof. As we file in we're told to unload our belongings. That's where we'll stay for the time being. We collapse on the bare floor. My mother says that we'd sleep well by taking turns on top of our belongings.

Yesterday after dark I ate something interesting. My sister Margit pressed it into my hand with a piece of bread. They call it bacon. But it's a sin to eat it. "There's nothing else now," Margit said. "You've got to live, and this stuff is made of a black pig and that's allowed," she lied.

There was an announcement a short time ago. We are forbidden to hide anything. For now, no one who tells about what he had hidden at home will be harmed. However, it gets out that some rich people who were taken home returned beaten black and blue. My sister Margit pulled me aside and stuffed a pair of earrings into my breast pocket. "That's our secret, little brother," she whispered. "Take care of them and mum's the word."

What's all the shouting about? "Detail! The camp commandant is coming! Attention! Everybody stands!"

They're in front of us. There are four of them. The leader has a whip in his hand. He's quite young, blond, and well dressed. His face is white and masklike as he looks around slowly. I think he must be the commandant. He yells something from time to time. Is it possible that only I don't understand what he's yelling? I don't think anyone is even breathing it's so quiet. A few steps behind the man with the whip, but stepping in unison with him, are three German soldiers. They clasp their machine guns with both hands.

I've never felt this way. Utter terror, I think. I must have caught it from the adults. Why are thousands of people terror-stricken? And why not those four in the middle?

At last, we're ready to move out. We're standing in rows of six. Why must we stand for so long? Why is it forbidden to talk? Perhaps the reason the csendőrök are gathering is because they'll escort us. Six of them line up facing us, the seventh is shouting orders. Suddenly they make an about-face. On orders they place their rifles on the ground. One of them goes off with a terrific bang.

We march and march. Falling behind can be very dangerous. "Look at Grandma," my mother whispers. "If she can hold up, a big young man like you can, too."

Finally we reach the train that will take us somewhere. Isn't it exciting? Ebes. That's the name of the little train station. It's really quite small. Two sets of rails pass in front of the station. Empty cattle cars stand on one of them—big, brown cars with their heavy sliding doors shut. Rozi says the reason they're called cattle cars is because cows are transported in them.

How desolate this place is! No one is here but us and the csendőrök. Well, we've all made it in good shape. My mother and older sisters alternated carrying my brother Lackó. He's only four, but a strong little boy because often he did not let them carry him.

It's a nice, sunny day as we stand in front of the open doors of the cattle cars. The csendőrök are nowhere to be seen. Let's peek into a car and see how we'll be traveling. There's a long iron gangplank—its bottom at level with my navel—to each cattle car and then the floor of the car at level with my head. There is no window, only an opening with bars over it. I hope it won't take long to get wherever we're going. It would be so nice to steal away and go home. The only problem is that no one is at home. Everybody is here.

What does that csendőr want here? He's a handsome man with a smiling face. "I only want to do good by you," the csendőr says. "The Germans could be very cruel, you know, if they find something valuable on you when you get there. You heard the order 'No valuables are permitted to leave the country.' If you happen to have any jewelry or money left with you this is your last chance to give it to me quickly and quietly."

Many say they have nothing left. I can see some of them are not telling the truth but I feel that under the circumstances it's not a sin. I'm lying, too, because my sister's earrings are stuffed in my breast pocket.

We're boarding the train at long last. Our place, measuring about a blanket and a half, is in a corner. All of us—Mom, Margit, Rozi, Kató, Lackó, Aunt Jolán, Grandma, and I—squat on it. The door is pulled shut. There's hardly any light in the car. We're packed in like sardines. You know, I'm embarrassed to do Number Two in that bucket in the corner that everybody uses and around which there are so many people. But how long can I hold back?

I have no idea where the train is headed. It's dark now, and it feels as if the train is moving in a different direction than it did during the day. The adults could look outside through that opening high up in the corner, but it's forbidden. If anyone tries to look, we've been told, he'll be shot at.

We get four slices of bread a day. If only I weren't so thirsty all the time. My mother brought a bottle of vinegar along. She tells me if I sip some I won't be thirsty. Have you ever tried sipping vinegar when you're thirsty? I've tried it and it tastes awful.

During the day I stretch out on the floor, thanks to my sisters. They stand so that I'll have enough room. My mother sits next to me, rocking my brother in her lap. She's humming a tune.

We've reached out destination. I feel dizzy and can hardly climb down from the cattle car. Margit helps me. Again we're counted. I hear shouts. We're ordered to line up alongside the train. The sun is blazing. An old woman won't be coming down. She's dead. I'd take a look but I'm scared.

Again, we have to wait. My stomach hurts. My mother says aside from being hungry, there's nothing wrong with me. I should sip some vinegar, she tells me. It'll keep me from being hungry. I hate even the sight of that bottle of vinegar.

The csendőrök are no longer around. Soldiers are watching us now. They don't speak Hungarian, yet they shout all the time. Rozi says we're in Austria, probably near Vienna.

We're led to a huge barracks. That's where we'll be staying. There are lots of people around but lots of bunk beds, too. I get a sleeping place of my very own.

The food tastes awful. My mother says it's real vegetables. We should be happy it's edible and warm and eat it even if it tastes awful. Margit says it's cattle turnip, therefore good for us.

According to my mother anything black and jumping is not a louse but a flea. Whatever it is we're on our way to the fumigating chamber.

I am very self-conscious about all this. I hardly know where to look. We now must stand stark naked in this large concrete-floor room. Women and girls, also stark naked, walk in and out all the time. We undress in the outer room. Each of us must put all of his belongings in the middle of a sheet, then make it into a sack by tying its four corners into a knot, and place it into an oven of sorts. Rozi tells me it'll be disinfected and returned soon.

There are more and more of us in the disinfecting room. All I can see are countless naked buttocks wherever I turn. I recognize members of my family only by their faces. Below the waist all people look almost alike.

It's my turn now. In groups of four we step into a smaller room. I've never seen such dense steam in my life. We're told to step under the shower heads and start washing ourselves. However, no one minds me, and I'm certainly not going to shower now on my own.

When everybody is finished we must go into another room. There's no steam there. One by one we must step in front of a man who has on a white coat and sits on a chair. He must be a doctor. Finally, he's through with me and I move on. At a counter my sister Margit pushes my sack to me. I don't think they did anything to it because it's knotted exactly the way I had it. "Get dressed, young man," Margit says.

We're put in another barracks. The adults say we won't stay long because we'll soon be taken to Vienna to work. The adults say I should be happy to be here. Compared to "some other places," where we are now is heaven. I don't understand adults.

Vienna is an unbelievably big city. The multistory buildings are large and somber, and the streets are wide and run forever. We march in tight formations, but I can see no guards escorting us. I think the reason we're so disciplined on our own is because we're in a foreign country, don't know anybody and are homeless, don't speak the language, have nothing to eat, and don't know what tomorrow will bring.

We stop, wait, and start out again. Suddenly the group in the front turns right, the rest must go on. It seems we won't all be in the same place. At last we turn into the horseshoe-shaped courtyard of a building. It's a school! A real school in Vienna! What an enormous assembly hall! On the first floor the rooms open to a corridor. I wonder if the second floor looks the same. Not a desk or even a podium in any of the classrooms—only iron bunk beds placed in a circle around a large table.

There are some twenty of us in this classroom, which will be our home for now. A four-tiered bunk bed in a corner is for all eight of my family. The beds are pushed together in pairs. A distance of hardly a meter (39 in) separates one pillow from the other. It's impossible to say where one family begins and another ends.

Things are beginning to take shape. There are lots of kids in the room. We get bread and butter. The adults have elected Mr. Steimetz to distribute the butter. He uses a knife to mold the butter in the shape of a cube. Now he's pressing lines on it with the help of a ruler. He wants to divide the butter into twenty-seven parts with mathematical precision. The best food on earth is bread and butter.

We are allowed to go into the courtyard. It's so big and has a lot of chestnut trees. We're not allowed to go out to the street, however. A soldier stands on the other side of the gate. We'll ask Margit what *"Tod"* means. That's what's written on the front of the soldier's cap. Imagine, Margit says that if I learn Austrian I'll be able to speak with the Germans, too.

A few days after we got settled in the school, which is in the Florisdorf District of Vienna, the able-bodied adult men were taken away to work in the morning. They returned in the evening. My mother and sisters worked at a nearby Shell Oil Company plant. Boys under ten were not allowed to work. But one day I heard that a group of ten workers was being assembled. When I saw they came up short, I went there and signed up.

"How old are you?" I was asked.

"I'll be ten," I answered, mumbling the first two words so they couldn't be heard. Thus I didn't lie. I was signed up as Tiberius Bauer and told that I'd start the next day.

In the evening when my mother found out what I had

done she was less than pleased. Of course, I neglected to tell her that I had volunteered. She was concerned that her little son would go to work on the other side of the city and asked everyone to keep an eye on me. All members of the group, except Ol' Number Ten, were adults.

A man came and escorted us so that we wouldn't get lost. We walked and took the streetcar, just like regular people.

For a long time now we've been working in District I on a house at 9 Kirner Strasse. I already know where to get on the streetcar, what number to transfer on. I always manage to get to our place of work and home on time.

I've gotten used to wearing the yellow star. Somehow I don't feel it is compulsory to wear it. It is like carrying identification papers. Hardly anyone talks to me anyway. When somebody does talk to or approach me, it's not with malicious intent. On the contrary, I've gotten used to not reacting even when I travel on the crowded streetcar and feel someone's hand in my pocket. I don't grab at it, for I usually end up with people putting things into my pocket rather than picking it. Often it's an apple or some other kind of food. I even got a bread ration ticket the other day.

Whatever food I get I take home. It makes my family happy and that makes me happy. They work much closer to home than I and cannot go around in the city as freely as I. So I've become the family's food supplier.

Today I did something stupid and I'm ashamed of what I did. It happened in the morning. I got off the last car of the train and as usual trudged by myself toward my place of work. As I was passing a butcher shop, I noticed that the butcher, a white-coated, chubby man, was standing in the doorway. He smiled and signaled to me to go in. I did just that. He wrapped a huge piece of salami in paper and handed it to me.

I love salami even though I am not allowed to eat it at

home as it is not kosher. I took a bite. It tasted great. All day I tried to even it out. Somehow it always looked crooked. Finally that piece of salami got to be so small that I was ashamed to take it home. So now I have pangs of conscience and an upset stomach at the same time.

The weather is freezing here in Vienna. Blocks of ice are floating in the Danube. My mother put layers of clothes on me. I'm wearing a pair of wooden-soled boots. They keep me warm because in addition to wearing socks I wrap my feet in newspaper and then pull on the boots.

I like to walk by myself. I can also purchase the weekly tram ticket, and for a ration ticket I can buy a whole loaf of bread, which I take home. The work isn't hard, either. A rectangular wooden pipe starts at the fifth floor and winds downward, ending at the street. Women carry all kinds of bricks to me and I place them into the pipe. I enjoy listening to the rumbling sounds the bricks make as they roll down the pipe. Down on the street an old Austrian man holding a shovel stands at the opening of the pipe. He separates the bricks as they hit the ground. The undamaged bricks he throws on one side, the fragments on the other.

Three months have passed. It's gotten warmer. They say it's spring. Our situation has changed little. However, the city is showing more signs of destruction. Virtually every day, at exactly eleven in the morning, the sirens start wailing and the bombing starts. There is hardly any food in the stores; you can't get any even for food tickets.

I still work at 9 Kirner Strasse. I don't feel so good. The trouble is there is no toilet where I work. Rather, there is one but it happens to be in the dark basement and I'm scared to go down there. What if I bump into a rat? I have to hold back Number Two—I don't always succeed even though I try hard—the whole day. I've been trying to get used to going to the toilet before leaving for work. I can put up with not being able to wash myself, but this thing . . .

I saved some food tickets, and on the way home I'll get a loaf of bread. It won't be easy to get it into the school. The commandant announced that it was forbidden to bring anything into the camp. Anyone caught trying would be punished. Somehow, I don't think he really means it, because yesterday after we got back home we had to stand in line for inspection. The loaf of bread I'd bought did not fit in my shoulder bag so I held it in my hand. When the commandant passed in front of me I held the loaf behind my back and when he passed behind my back I held it in front of me. Even though he never stopped talking in German he made no mention of the bread, so I ended up keeping it.

The sirens are sounding. It's ten minutes past eleven. They're late today. Let's go down into the air-raid shelter. There are very few of us wearing yellow stars in the shelter. Most of the people are locals. They're nice to us and have not chased us out of here. Everybody is so glum. Are they scared? The waves of attack come one after the other and closer and closer. If the building collapses Mom won't even know where to start looking for me.

At last the sirens are sounding again. It's in an even tone now, signaling the end of the air raid. We can go back to work. Better yet, we're going to have lunch. It's noon already. I haven't shown you where we get lunch, have I? It's not too far. I don't know why the tram isn't coming—let's walk.

Look over there! Only half of every house on the other side of the street is standing. Their fronts have collapsed. The whole street is covered with rubble. It's strange to see apartments cut in half. Those on top of one another must have been kitchens. You can still see plates in different colors on the walls. And there's even a cupboard. I hope it won't fall because just below it three helmeted men are pulling up pieces of rubble. What could they be looking for?

A fat lady stands there with a suitcase, sobbing loudly and wiping her eyes with a handkerchief. There's a huge swastika on her chest. I've never seen anything like that. Well, we've got yellow stars on our chests. Let's not feel sorry for her, shall we? Let's move on.

Here we are. That's where we'll have lunch. There are a lot of people here today. The line is formed on the street. No lunch today? I didn't realize how much damage the bombing has caused.

Somehow I have the feeling that the house we work on will never be finished. Yesterday four of us were suddenly taken to work in Döbling in the mental hospital. Margit says that it was home to Count István Széchenyi, that famous Hungarian, until he died. We had to load heavy planks on the three-wheeled truck. A little hunchbacked man kept shouting into our ears. When we were done, he ordered us to climb on top of the planks. The whole time I thought I'd fall off at any moment. The junky truck bounced all the way and there was nothing I could hang on to. When the truck stopped we had to unload the planks.

Today we're at 9 Kirner Strasse again. In the course of clearing the rubble I had the scare of my life. Suddenly what looked like pieces of red plaster rumbled in my direction. I jumped as far as I could. However, just as quickly I realized they were not pieces of red plaster but real Jonathan apples. Somebody had dropped a bunch of apples from above. Meanwhile, not one apple could be found in the stores anywhere.

Well, it had to happen sooner or later. We got caught in an air raid while still at home. We march down into the basement of the school. It's very crowded. We just stand, surrounded by a lot of people.

It's a strange kind of bombing. I can hear whistling sounds followed by small explosions. Fire! Fire! Everybody, run for your life! Some of us run into the street through the burning wooden doors. The building across the street from ours is on fire. The heat is unbearable. There are smaller fires all around. Brass shells, as thick as my arm, are all over the place. Phosphorus bombs, I think. The streets are deserted. Where are we going to go? The school is not on fire, only the doors. Let's dash back.

This whole thing feels like a very long vacation. For a year I haven't been going to school or the *cheder*. For a year I haven't had a book in my hands, written as much as a line, or studied even a minute. At times I'm depressed. Margit, my sister, says I'm reacting to the situation we're in. She's very smart. I really don't understand what she means but she must be right.

They say the Russians are getting closer. We're taken out of Vienna. We're put together with other groups. Our new place is also a school. It is getting more and more crowded. We're assigned to the assembly hall. There is hardly any room to stretch out comfortably on the stone floor. At night those who sleep are stepped on by those who stumble in the direction of the toilet. I hope it won't last long.

The adults are confused. They say that those with large families will be taken to Bergen Belsen and those able to work will dig trenches when the front gets here. But who will decide who is good for what?

I feel only bitterness and hunger. I don't know if the camp where we are now staying is the same as the one in which we lived when we arrived. I don't think we're far from Vienna. There are many barracks with barren, sandy patches of land among them. No trees, no plants anywhere. Far beyond the barbed-wire fence a forest is visible. My sisters say we're lucky because the Germans have no time for us.

It's quiet. There is hardly anything to eat. I'm always hungry. Margit says it's for my own good. I won't have a big stomach and the girls will like me.

I can hear the rumbling of guns all the time. They say the Russians are quite close. The German soldiers no longer guard us.

Unfortunately our luck has run out. Suddenly a group of

German soldiers shows up to escort us to the train station. We pack our belongings quickly and line up with our bags in front of the barracks. We must be going to another camp.

The adults look desperate. Mother says it would be a miracle if we were liberated here. I don't mind that we're going to a bigger camp. We'll have more to eat there. But I don't let anyone know what I'm thinking. I feel it is better to be liberated when one isn't hungry.

We've arrived at the station. Waiting for us are empty cattle cars. I know them only too well. A lot of people are shoved into each car. Then a soldier pulls the sliding doors shut. Again we're crowded into a corner. We're not going anywhere, perhaps for some time, because the sirens of the station have been sounded. The planes fly over, screaming. That's not unusual. However, what's unusual is the sound of anti-aircraft guns coming from the station.

Then everything is quiet again. I can hear only whistling sounds fading away. Suddenly there is a big bang. We're jostled back and forth in the car. The anti-aircraft guns are firing, too. Again those whistling sounds. Mom pulls a blanket over our heads. We're crouching on the floor of the cattle car with heads so close that our noses almost touch.

At last the blanket is off our heads. Margit says that the air-raid blanket was a good idea of Mom's. We're still not moving. The door is slid open. Apparently we're staying for the time being.

Nobody knows anything. What happened to the soldiers? Were they killed by the bombs or did they simply leave? Some people are getting off the cattle car and walking toward the barracks. Then suddenly everybody is getting off the train. Let's hurry so we won't lose our sleeping places.

The camp is quiet. No guards, no food. We've invented a terrific game. We sit in a circle in the sand and everyone tells about his favorite food. But he must tell about it slowly so the rest can imagine what it tastes like. Whenever it's my turn I tell about the cheese pockets my mother used to make for breakfast. They were shaped like beautiful big bags, glittering and golden brown from the icing and filled with white cottage cheese that was visible in its four corners. A terrific game, isn't it?

I've suspected for some time that Rozi and Margit, my older sisters, sneak out of the camp after dark in search of food. But they haven't brought anything back recently.

Suddenly I can hear the sound of approaching planes. I turn around only to catch a glimpse of small planes swooping down. I can even make out the pilot in one of them. Suddenly lightning strikes from his propeller. It sounds like a machine gun. But he's not firing at me because he's already flown over me. It looks as if he's aiming at the people moving along by the forest. The planes leave as fast as they came. It's quiet again.

If things stay as they are, we'll make it. The adults discover that some of the train cars that had been hit contain food. Some of the adults are preparing to get near the train after it gets dark.

Take a look at that! Crystal sugar. And how much of it! That's all we've got for now. My sisters could've brought back apricot preserves, too, but they didn't have a container with them. They said the adults crowded the barrel that contained the preserves so much that some of them nearly fell into it.

The adults are getting bolder and bolder in sneaking out to the train. Yesterday they brought back military uniforms and boots. But they're going to be sorry! German soldiers have arrived. An officer is entering the barracks, accompanied by two soldiers with machine guns. He's screaming; everybody else is quiet. The officer wants a translator. He's searching for those boots. I happened to see where our neighbors had hid them. Nobody moves or says anything. I guess they're afraid to return the boots. If the situation weren't so serious it would even make a good game. I cannot help but smile faintly at the thought of it. The officer noticed it. He steps in front of me and starts yelling. Mother comes over, her face ashen, and points to my head as if she wanted to say, "That child isn't normal." Finally the German soldiers depart. "Why do you do such things to me, son?" my mother asks. I can't think of an answer but I do feel sorry for her.

It was a few days ago that I first saw Russian soldiers. I was loafing around in front of our barracks. It was quiet. The soldiers were already a few yards from me when I noticed them. There were only two, carrying machine guns. They wore wrinkled earth-colored coats and round fur hats. Both looked exhausted and underfed. The short one's head was bandaged with gleaming white gauze.

When the soldiers reached me they stopped. "Nyemecz? Nyemecz?" (Russian for "German.") they asked, looking around. I pointed to the yellow star on my chest and shook my head. Then they walked on and soon disappeared. I ran inside. "Mom! Mom! I've seen two Russian soldiers. Are we liberated now?"

We're all alike, dirty and hungry. The principal says the front has moved on. We should move, too—homeward, otherwise we'll starve to death. The adults agree. Groups are formed according to place of origin and destination. We, of course, would like to return to Debrecen. Father might be at home already. Also, Feri, Margit's husband, will look for us there. He's a forced labor serviceman. They were married a few months before he was taken away.

The adults have gotten hold of a wagon. There's room for two horses on each side of the shaft of the wagon, but we haven't got even one horse. The wagon itself is an ordinary contraption made of wood. It has sides that fold down and average-size wheels with wooden spokes. They'll roll well on the hard-surfaced streets.

So many bags are loaded on the wagon that hardly any room is left for the elderly and the children. There must be about forty of us, arguing as many ways. Some take offense and join other groups.

In early morning we're ready to move out. The wagon, however, is not. Lots of people are pushing it. It won't budge.

Half of the bags are thrown off and everybody gets off, too. Slowly the wagon is moving. The principal says all we have to do is go 500 kilometers (310 mi) and we're at home. Perhaps we'll be able to transfer to a train.

The wagon, carrying only a grandmother and a baby, crawls at a snail's pace. It's tough to push it. We must catch horses. From time to time we see some, wandering and seemingly deserted. We try to catch one but it runs away. We'll try again tomorrow. It's getting dark. Even though everybody is scared, we'll sleep in the open field.

It took us two weeks to reach Bratislava. During the journey my older sisters always had to be watched so that our liberators wouldn't take them to "peel a few potatoes." By day they dressed up to look like old women and smeared dirt on their faces. At night we were their bodyguards. Wherever we stopped, mostly at roadside houses, about twenty of us slept on the floor in empty rooms. The girls slept by the wall and we lay our heads on them as if they were pillows.

As we moved through a village shortly before we reached Bratislava, a group of Russian soldiers stood in front of a big house, leaning against the fence. They watched us pass by in the middle of the street. Suddenly one of them started walking toward me. He must have been an officer, judging by the stars on his epaulet. When he reached me he pulled out a knife and with a determined, swift gesture he cut off my yellow star. Then he turned and walked back to his unit with my yellow star in his hand. It happened so fast—and without one word uttered—that I could hardly comprehend the true meaning of the act. Suddenly I felt I had been deprived of something.

In Bratislava we received food and soon were on our way home, now by train—of course on a cattle train, but with the doors of the cars open. A ticket taker even came around to collect the fare. We had no money to pay for tickets, but my sisters solved the problem by arguing with him. On our way somehow Mom found out that Dad was alive and already had a tinman's shop on Hatvan Street in Debrecen.

It was at the beginning of May in 1945 that we arrived in Debrecen. The small train station was at the end of Hatvan Street. We set out to find my father's shop. It was at the corner of Pást Street. Mom sent in my five-year-old brother by himself. I watched him enter the shop.

My father was a short man who wore very thick glasses and, as always, a hat on his head. He looked up as the door opened and then down at the little blond boy who quietly stood in front of him. I could see, above his glasses, that tears filled his eyes.

For me it was then that the war ended.

In 1946 Tibor Bauer was a member of a Zionist youth group that prepared to leave for Palestine. However, his parents prevented him from going. In 1949 he and some of his relatives tried to leave Communist Hungary illegally for Israel, but they were arrested at the border between Hungary and Czechoslovakia and jailed for three days. Then he moved to Budapest and graduated from the Jewish High School in 1953. The following year he began his studies in electrical engineering at the Technical University. During the Revolution of 1956 he made a third attempt to leave the country but was again arrested by Soviet soldiers at the border and returned to Budapest. Since graduating from the Technical University he has worked as an electrical engineer, mostly in managerial positions. He and his wife, Martha Hentz, whom he met while both were students in the Jewish High School, have two daughters and live in Budapest.

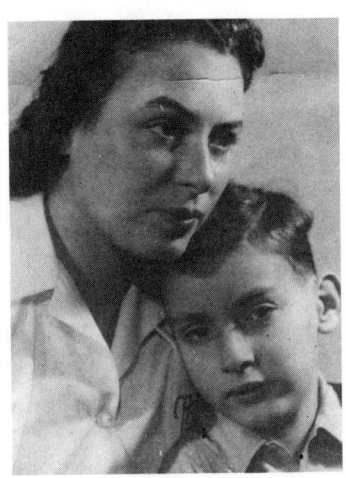

PETER TARJAN

THANK YOU, RAOUL WALLENBERG

I was the only child of my parents who around 1930 moved from Pécs, a city 105 miles (165 km) south of Budapest, to Budapest, where I was born in 1936. My family lived in an apartment building in a predominantly Jewish neighborhood in District VII. As were other able-bodied Jewish men, my father was called for paramilitary work as a forced laborer *(munkaszolgálatos)* many times between 1941 and 1944. He was usually let go after a few days or weeks because he was employed by a tanning factory that claimed his services were essential for the war effort. After the German invasion on March 19, 1944, our relatively comfortable stituation changed drastically, just as it changed for all other Jews in Hungary. From that point on my father did forced labor most of the time. In the summer of 1944 our apartment building was selected to house only Jews. At about the same time we lost contact with our relatives in and around Pécs. My maternal grandparents, aunts, uncles, and cousins on both sides were deported to Auschwitz.

Swiss *Schutzpasses*, or protective documents, began to pop up all over the city that summer. My parents got at least three sets of papers, probably all forgeries. Such passes stated that the person or family named in the document was under the protection of a neutral country's government, and requested the authorities to treat the protected person as they would a citizen of that neutral country. In some cases it was stated that the person would be resettled in the issuing country as soon as the war came to an end.

On several occasions my mother was also taken away to do forced labor, but she was allowed to return home to take care of me. I was then eight years old. In November, armed with our Schutzpasses we moved into one of the Swiss protected houses at 25 St. Stephen Park in the international ghetto on the bank of the Danube. We walked there with my mother's friend Jolán, and her two-year-old daughter, Trudi. We were accompanied by an armed soldier who had been hired by Jolán to protect us from arrest or harassment during this trek. In early December, Arrow Cross men (Hungarian Fascists, *nyilasok* or *nilaskeresztesek*), entered our crowded building and ordered all women who had children above the age of two to gather in the backyard. It was then and there that I last saw my mother, from the window on the sixth floor as she was lined up with the other women in the backyard.

My mother left me with Jolán. I don't know what arrangements they had made, if any. Jolán turned me over— along with some money, I suspect—to a military tailor who was a Christian. He took me to various orphanages in the city, hoping to leave me in one. But as they were all overcrowded, he was unsuccessful. He then took me to the Budapest ghetto, where he located Ágnes, my mother's sister. Ágnes told me years later that she did not want to keep me there because there was no food, a typhus epidemic was starting, and she had heard rumors that the ghetto was being mined in order to be destroyed.

The tailor took me back to his shop and hid me in the loft. Every evening he locked me up in the shop. I was not permitted to move around or make the slightest noise. After a few days he was able to leave me at an International Red Cross orphanage that had just been established in an apartment near the Western Railway Station. I was assigned to a room that was home to about ten boys, some of them teenagers. I think I was the second youngest. The orphanage was run by a Mr. Fogarasi, but I am not sure of the name. It was probably an assumed one. As I recall, he seemed somewhat younger than my father, who was forty at that time.

After a few days I had a visitor. It was Panni, my mother's friend. I do not know how she had learned of my whereabouts, and I don't think she remembers either. She told me that she and her mother were in a Swedish protected house at 4 Tátra Street. She would have taken me in, but she was sharing a single room with eighteen or nineteen relatives— her aunts and uncles, a retarded teenage cousin, and another young male cousin who was suffering from dysentery. Panni told me that if everything else failed, I should go to her place nonetheless.

A few days had passed and there were rumors of evacuation of the orphanage. There were also vague stories about how the Arrow Cross men took Jews to the Danube and executed them. One evening Mr. Fogarasi called us into his office, one at a time. He asked me if there was any place where I could go because the orphanage was going to be evacuated. He might have spoken to Panni during her earlier visit. He told me that he had made arrangements with the superintendent of the building to let us out after dark, one at a time. I packed my small suitcase and was ready to leave.

The super made me stand at the courtyard end of the long tunnel-shaped entrance. He must have been watching what was going on in the street. He finally signaled to me.

In a moment I was out on the broad sidewalk of one of the main boulevards. It was just a few days before Christmas and a lot of people crowded the streets. I don't remember for sure, but I think my Jewish star had been cut from my coat. I was probably quite a conspicuous sight, a little boy alone with a small suitcase. The streetlights had been turned on, and some stores stayed open despite the Red Army, which was just outside the city. Either I had realized that I was lost and asked a woman for directions, or she stopped me to find out what I was doing. I think it was the latter. At any event, I did not want to tell her anything about what I was doing or who I was because I had been instructed by my parents and everyone else to be discreet with strangers at all times.

The woman was insistent, and she took me to the address I had with me. It was only a few minutes walk in the direction of the Danube. We found the front gate locked and the superintendent uncooperative. Eventually he relented and contacted Panni. Years later Panni told me that the super was willing to let me stay in the building only for the night, but Panni somehow managed to extend my one-night stay until our liberation by the Russians some four weeks later.

The building was one of many under Swedish protection in the neighborhood. A few years ago I read in one of the books that Raoul Wallenberg had an apartment in the adjacent building. He and his driver had left from there by car, hoping to make contact with the Russians, around January 12, 1945.

I remember the air raids and the door-to-door fighting. Even though everybody else did, Panni, Béla, her uncle, and I never went to the cellar during air raids. Panni never told me, but I think it was because I was there against the wishes of the superintendent. Instead, she told me that it was because the cellar was unbearably smelly and depressing.

The windows were all broken from the pressure of the bombing. We had a clear view of a balcony across the street, where we first saw a German machine gunner firing toward the boulevard. Later Russian soldiers were doing exactly the same thing. We saw one of the Russians getting shot and then being dragged into the apartment. A few moments later another Russian took his place.

The only source of heat in the bitter cold was a tiny stove on which we had a huge pot of cold water with whole dry peas soaking. The fire was out. After the peas had swollen in the water, we sat around the pot and shelled the peas. We thought that the shells were not only indigestible but would somehow make us all sick. When all the peas were shelled, someone lit the fire in the stove, and the peas were cooked without salt or anything. Boiled pea mush was all the food we had. We ate it every day even though it tasted awful. Panni seems to remember that Wallenberg's people from the next building gave a slice of bread to each child, but I distinctly remember the excitement of having the first piece of gooey cornbread about a week after our liberation. We divided about a pound of bread among us. I had almost forgotten the taste of bread by then.

Raoul Wallenberg had indeed saved my life by creating a haven for thousands of Jews, including Panni's family, in Swedish protected houses. He was also instrumental in establishing the international ghetto where my mother and I had been able to stay earlier. Finally, he had saved the life of my aunt Ágnes by preventing the demolition of the ghetto. Wallenberg's activities in Budapest are well documented. Had I stayed with Ágnes in the ghetto, he would have provided for me another escape route from death if needed. Months or years later I learned that some of the children from my orphanage were taken to the ghetto, where some survived; others were taken to the Danube and shot or shoved into the icy water.

My parents never returned from their separate routes. A friend of my grandparents claimed to have seen my mother in Mauthausen. She was weak and ill. My father had sent a postcard to our old address. It was dated March 1945, and postmarked at a Budapest train station. He wrote that he was going to see us soon. Whether it was written earlier and mailed by someone else, I shall never know. Another possibility is that he did indeed survive and return to Budapest, where he was rounded up by the Russians along with thousands of other men and taken into labor camps in various parts of the Soviet Union. Many of these men returned to Hungary several years later. One of them was even permitted to write a book about his experiences.

Of all the relatives from Pécs only my father's sister, Böske, and a second cousin of my mother's returned from Auschwitz. From the neighboring towns and villages a few cousins survived.

Until a few years ago I knew very little about Raoul Wallenberg, except that he had been responsible for saving many Jewish lives, including mine, in Hungary. I knew that there was a street named after him near the site of the international ghetto, and there is a plaque in his honor on the wall of one of the buildings on that street. The plaque, however, gives no clues as to his fate other than that he had disappeared during the siege of Budapest in January 1945. When I realized that my life was saved by him, I started searching for material about him, but it did not seem urgent, since I thought that he had died in 1945.

In January 1985, I had some time to spend at a library in Miami, where I found two books about him. I started reading *The Righteous Gentile* by John Bierman. I suddenly realized that the night I was reading it was exactly forty years after Wallenberg had left to meet Soviet Marshal Malinovsky. The book gave January 12, 1945, as the date of Wallenberg's departure. It was a very strange feeling to realize that the man might still be alive in some terrible Soviet prison. I have read a lot about him since then. I have also gone back to Hungary in search of additional information on him at Budapest's Széchenyi Library.

For the first time since my departure from Hungary I also visited the building at 25 St. Stephen Park, from which my mother was taken. I recognized it instantly. I remembered well the details of the entrance and the courtyard, which, however, looked much smaller. I had grown up since then. The superintendent came out of her apartment and asked me what or whom I was looking for. Ágnes, who was with me, said that I was looking for memories. "Oh," the woman said, "I understand. That happens quite often here." We also visited Tátra Street. The gray and worn old buildings were still a permanent part of my memory. I saw the balcony from which the machine guns were fired and the door in the apartment. The entrance from the square that I had not seen in forty-two years was familiar. All I can say is that children do remember!

Thank you, Raoul Wallenberg, for two things. First, for saving our lives—mine, Panni's, her family's, and Ágnes's. Second, for enabling me to answer without hesitation the question: "Whom do you admire the most among the living or the dead?"

I do not have any other real heroes.

After the Soviet armies liberated Hungary, Peter Tarjan left Budapest to live with an aunt in a small town. Eventually he returned to Budapest, finished high school, and in 1954 became a student of electrical engineering at the Technical University. During the Revolution of 1956 he participated in anti-Soviet and anti-Communist activities. After the Soviet forces crushed the revolution, he left Hungary and came to the United States. He continued his studies, receiving his M.S. from MIT and Ph.D. from Syracuse University. Dr. Tarjan and his wife, Susanna, a law student, have two sons, Joshua and Aaron. Dr. Tarjan is professor and chairman of the Department of Biomedical Engineering at the University of Miami.

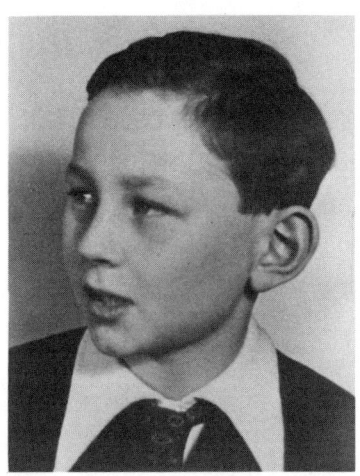

GEORGE S. PICK

DO YOU BELIEVE IN MIRACLES?

A few days ago my friend Judy and I walked in the nearby park enjoying Washington's Indian Summer. We discussed politics, science, and religion. I don't remember what prompted me to ask her whether or not she believed in miracles. Judy is a scientist who believes that everything has a rational explanation. I told her that I believed in personal miracles and related to her my own story, which took place during the last year of the Second World War, when I was ten years old, in Budapest, Hungary, in 1945.

Are there miracles? Judge for yourself.

"Look at the sky," exclaimed Uncle John. I looked up into the cloudless blue space above my head.

It was a morning in June 1944. What I saw was hundreds of silver airplanes moving across the vast sky.

"How could you be afraid?" asked Uncle John.

But I was. I looked at my watch. It was eleven o'clock in the morning. I tugged on Uncle John's coat.

"Let us go back to the bomb shelter. The sirens signaled an air raid ten minutes ago."

We retreated into the basement shelter. The rest of the people who lived in the apartment building were there already.

Uncle John was a kindly man in his thirties. He was the superintendent in the building we lived in. He had a son my age, and he and his family were the only Christians who lived in our building. The rest of us were Jewish. The house was a "starred" building. It was only a few blocks away from where we had lived for ten years on Queen Elizabeth Street until the German Army occupied Hungary and ordered us, like many hundreds of thousands of Jews, out of our homes and into the "starred" buildings.

That happened in June 1944.

We were lucky. My maternal grandmother's two sisters and their families lived only a few blocks away from us on Columbus Street. Their building had been declared a "starred" residence. So my mother, grandmother, and I moved in with my grandmother's younger sister, Great-Aunt Gizella, her daughter, Elizabeth, and her son, Tibor. They had shared a small one-bedroom apartment in a three-story yellow stucco building since before the war.

So, now six people lived in the apartment. My father and cousin Tibor came home to spend the night with us occasionally. The place was wall-to-wall beds and convertible sofas. It looked like a furniture warehouse. There was not much room to move around.

Why was our building called a "starred" house? you ask.

Well, on the front, above the main entrance, was a big yellow star to show that only Jews lived there. The entrance to the building and its grounds was always locked. It was

Uncle John's responsibility to make sure that we did not get out during curfew. He was our jailer. Curfew started at five in the afternoon and lasted until ten in the morning. When we went shopping we had to wear a yellow star on our outer garments. Many stores had large signs saying that they would not serve or sell anything to Jews. If we were caught on the street during curfew or without the yellow star, we could be severely punished, jailed, or worse. Despite all these restrictions my mother managed to get us enough food so we did not starve.

There were no children of my age in the apartment house except Uncle John's son, but he was not allowed to play with me. An only child, I always lived among adults, and got used to playing alone. And that is what I did most of the time on Columbus Street.

These were the circumstances under which we lived on Columbus Street in the spring and summer of 1944.

I had my tenth birthday nine days after the German Army occupied Hungary. I understood much of what was happening. My father had been inducted into a forced labor brigade for Jewish men. They shipped him out of Budapest in early April and he was assigned to road construction. He was not used to the heavy physical work required in breaking up large boulders into medium-size gravel with nothing more than steel hammers and wedges. His unit was stationed fifty miles (80.5 km) from Budapest.

By May something new entered our lives with terrifying regularity: bombing raids—twice a day, at eleven o'clock in the morning and at nine at night. We lived on the second floor and it took us a few minutes to walk down to the basement air-raid shelter. The raids lasted from a few minutes to hours and regulated our lives. We had our lunch and dinner so that the raids wouldn't catch us in the middle of meals. After our supper the adults in my family played either cards or with the Ouija board. I bet you don't know what a Ouija board is. Let me explain. First, there is a large board that has all the letters of the alphabet written on it. This board is placed on the table. On the top of it we put an ordinary drinking glass, upside-down. Each of the three or more people playing touched the bottom of the glass with two fingers and asked a question from someone whom we all knew—someone famous who was dead. The theory was that the spirit of the dead would move the glass and spell out the answer. Do you believe it?

At night our windows were covered with black paper so that the light in the apartment would not be visible outside. In fact, we checked for stray light every night since it was punishable by heavy jail terms (and later by execution). The city was pitch dark at night.

When all of us were in the air-raid shelter, the heavy steel doors were locked from the inside. These doors—one opened to the garden and one to the stairway—were to protect us against blast, debris, and even against gas attacks. But they had no acoustic insulation. So the sounds of bombs falling, a very high-pitched noise, and the blasts, were amplified.

At eleven in the morning on that fateful Friday, June 2, 1944, we all sat there in a dimly lit room, everyone very quiet, as if silence would help us hide from the bombs. For the first ten or fifteen minutes we only heard muffled blasts from far away. Then, an ear-piercing whistling sound was getting louder and louder. Then, a shattering blast. The building rocked as if it had been hit by an earthquake. The lights went out. From the outside a brilliant flash of light appeared around the frame of the steel door. There was screaming in the shelter. I crawled on my mother's lap and she put her hands over my ears. It was quiet for a few minutes and then there was a larger, earth-shattering whistle followed by a chorus of screams from the people. Pieces of concrete fell from the ceiling. I was shaking and crying. My mother tried to calm me down. We sat there in pitch dark. There was another blast and still another.

The raid lasted for three hours, then it was over. We survived. The sirens sounded the end of the raid. We stumbled out of the shelter and into the yard. What we saw was unbelievable. On the right side of the building there had been four tennis courts. Now there was a huge crater perhaps 15 feet (4.5 m) deep and 30 to 35 feet (9 to 10.5 m) in diameter. The dirt around the rim piled up another 8 to 10 (2 to 3 m) feet. Across the street, where a two-story private villa had stood that morning, there was a similar crater. Fifteen people had lived in the villa.

Behind our building there had been a six-story apartment building. Only its main fire wall was still standing. The rest of the building was a heap of rubble. On the fourth floor a bathtub hung in a crazy angle in midair, held by pipes and pieces of the fire wall. On the fifth floor some pictures were still attached to the wall, but the floors and ceiling were not there anymore. Remnants of living rooms and bedrooms, and pieces of yellow and purple wallpaper were visible on the only wall still standing.

There was a stench in the air and the smell of fire. The sky around us was full of smoke, and the purple reflection of the blaze was visible in every direction. We went upstairs and found our room covered with glass. All the windows of the building had been shattered by the blast of the bombs. We began the cleanup. There was no electricity or gas, and the water trickled for a few minutes, then it stopped. Over loudspeakers we heard the order: A twenty-four-hour curfew for Jews. Violators would be arrested.

Later that evening we heard over a battery-operated radio that more than one-third of the city was in ruins. Railroad terminals, railroad stations, large factories, and electrical generator plants were especially hard hit. Thousands had died. But there were no paratroopers and there was no fighting in the streets. Our dream of the liberation was far away (and in fact would not happen for seven and a half months).

The rest of the summer was uneventful for me. We found out several weeks later that the Allies had landed in Europe on June 6, 1944, just four days after that massive bombing of Budapest.

We had another saturation attack early in September, but it hit a different part of the city, so we were not as affected as in June. A wonderful thing happened to us about this time. My father's labor unit moved close to Budapest, and he came home two or three times a week. He risked his life, because it was illegal for a Jewish forced laborer to be on the street after dark and before dawn. But my father removed his yellow armband and came, taking a chance that if caught he would be severely punished or even shot. He only slept four to five hours and had to leave about four in the morning. Uncle John, the super, unlocked the entrance to the building when my father came home at night and left in the morning. My father bribed him with considerable sums. But even with bribes few Christians took a chance to do anything for the Jews. If it was found out that they helped Jews, the Christians would also be subjected to jail and even possible execution. So, we were thankful to Uncle John for helping my father, even if he took money for it.

Then events started moving rapidly. On October 15, 1944, Admiral Horthy, the regent of Hungary, read a proclamation on the radio that Hungary had concluded a secret peace treaty with the Soviet Union and declared neutrality. He ordered the armed forces of Hungary to cease firing and lay down their arms. We were ecstatic. We were free! We ran to the streets and took off our yellow stars. But the residents of neighboring houses were laughing and shouting, "You dirty Jews! You will all be dead like your brothers from the provinces."

Then the regular program on the radio was abruptly switched off and field music was blaring everywhere. From time to time terse announcements were made ordering units and army commanders to Budapest. By early afternoon it was clear that the effort of the more moderate elements in the government to make separate peace had failed. The Arrow Cross, the party of the most fanatical Hungarian Fascists, took over the government and seized power. They were helped by the SS and the Gestapo of the Nazis.

We were scared. Martial law was declared. This meant that if a Jew was caught without a yellow star, or after curfew, he or she was subject to execution on the spot. Groups of young boys (fourteen to eighteen years old) with submachine guns roamed the streets and stopped anyone of whom they were suspicious, demanding identification papers. The person who could not produce them was doomed.

My father still came home a few times a week. Then, in the last week of October he came home with news that the labor brigade was ordered to depart the very next morning. Their commander, one of the Righteous Gentiles, gave everyone a twenty-four-hour furlough and told the brigade that anyone who had a place to hide himself should do so, because whoever returned the next day would be transported to Germany. My father decided to go into hiding with a friend of his from the same labor brigade. They planned to meet later that afternoon and hide in the basement of a bombed-out home not far from where we lived. Father didn't think the war could last more than a couple of weeks. The Russian Army was less than 70 miles (112 k) away from Budapest.

We tearfully parted and my father was gone. He had forbidden us to tell his hiding place to anyone, including our relatives. Only my mother and I knew about it.

Two weeks went by. Still, the war was far from over. We had our two daily air raids. Then, one rainy morning, an armed Hungarian soldier knocked on our door. That was most unusual. He took my mother and me into the stairwell and gave us a note. It was from Father! His note was short, "Take some food and warm clothing. Don't tell anyone, including Grandmother, where you are going. Come at once to 6 Csángó Street." Our destination was in the middle of a low-class neighborhood of factories and slum buildings quite far from our part of the city.

My mother was apprehensive. She did not want to leave my grandmother (her mother) and felt that things were quiet in our neighborhood. So we did not pack anything, but we did go to the Csángó Street address to explain to my father that we were safe on Columbus Street. My father was upset and firmly told my mother to go home and do as she was told.

We got home only one hour before the curfew. My mother packed as fast as she could, and we were ready to leave in half an hour. Then we heard shouts and curses from the ground floor. Three men wearing Arrow Cross uniforms came in to search the house. They were young; one was no more than fifteen years old. Each carried a submachine gun. They came into our apartment, untied our packs, and threw everything on the floor, broke everything breakable, and then stormed out. They went from apartment to apartment and stole everything they thought had any value, mindlessly smashing furniture and ripping clothes. After about an hour of vandalizing they left.

My mother frantically packed once more. But by then the curfew had begun. Mother begged Uncle John to let us out of the building. After some money changed hands he let us out. We removed our yellow stars and took a streetcar. If we got caught we would be shot.

It was a long, long ride. Finally, after what seemed like hours, we got back to 6 Csángó Street. When we arrived, the place was completely dark from the outside. The building was surrounded by high walls topped with barbed wire. We had to pass through a heavy steel door. The same soldier who brought my father's note greeted us and let us in. The building was a two-story factory with large windows. One part of the structure had been hit by a bomb, and an entire corner of the building was on the ground in a large heap of concrete and twisted metal rubble. The large rooms in the building had long worktables and benches in the middle, and on the tables hundreds of Hungarian army uniforms were piled up. It was in the main room that we met my father. He was greatly relieved when he saw us. Then he told us the following remarkable story about how he got in the place.

He was to meet his friend at a prearranged place at a certain time. My father arrived on time and waited an hour, but his friend did not show up. After the war we learned that he had been caught in a dragnet and was killed by the Hungarian militia.

My father was desperate. He did not want to go back to his unit, which he felt was doomed, but he did not want to stay alone in the original hideout. He finally decided to seek help from some business acquaintances. He had three business partners over the years—two Christians and a Jew. My father went to their offices and found the two Christian partners cooperative and anxious to help. They told my father to go to a certain address, which was a textile factory where uniforms were manufactured for the Hungarian army. They told him to hand a note, in an envelope, to the commanding officer, a man by the name of Lieutenant Rázsó.

My father went to 6 Csángó Street and handed the envelope to the soldier guarding the door. He came back shortly and led my father to the office of Lieutenant Rázsó. And there he was—in full army uniform, including a sidearm—my father's third business partner, the Jewish one. He explained that the "uniform factory" was a front for a hiding place for about sixty Jewish forced laborers who, like my father, had deserted. Even the guard was a deserter (a Christian deserter from the army, not a Jewish forced laborer).

The place was sparsely lit inside, but I could see that there were women and children there as well. My father explained that many of the women and children were the wives and children, and even the parents, of the men hiding there. However, there was also a large group of young women who had been pulled out of railroad transports by escaped forced laborers operating as a rescue group. This group consisted of five or six young men in their twenties. Dressed in Arrow Cross uniforms and equipped with submachine guns and false papers, these death-defying heroes had rescued at least fifty people by the time we arrived. During our stay they brought in an additional twenty to thirty people.

There was no place to sleep except on the floor. We placed army uniforms under us and my mother and I used my father's overcoat for a blanket. In fact, that overcoat was our blanket for the next two months. My mother was very apprehensive about my grandmother and other relatives whom we had left behind.

We did not know the fate of my grandmother and the other relatives until the war was over. But this is what happened. Early the morning after we had left, the Arrow Cross men came back and took everybody to the brickyards, which had been converted into a transit camp. Uncle John knew where my relatives were taken and was able to get in contact with my grandmother's brother, who was under the protection of the Swedish embassy. He contacted Raoul Wallenberg, who helped my grandmother and great-aunts. All the others who lived in the building, young and old, were ordered to walk toward the western part of the country in one of the many death marches. None survived.

In the next few days after our arrival, the men built large, three-level bunkbeds in the factory. After that it was easier to sleep. We got three places on the mid-level of the bunkbeds in the largest of the five rooms. After a few days we started to meet people. There was a boy my age, John. We played together a lot. A young woman, Kató, became my friend. We talked for hours about "adult" things. I was ten, she twenty-two. I think she preferred the company of a young man named Andrew, who was closer to her age. I was sort of jealous of him. Anyway, they bunked close together, and after the children went to sleep, the adults stayed up and played cards and games. So, Kató and Andrew had ample opportunity to talk.

Food was brought in and we had enough to eat. The factory, however, was unheated. It was cold in November 1944.

The days went by quietly, although I was frightened by the air raids. The factory had no shelter, so we just stayed on the first floor during the daytime raids and tried to sleep through the night raids. During the second week of December, disaster struck. At about 10 A.M. we heard loud shouts from the yard in front of the factory buildings. A group of five to six men in civilian clothes but with guns in their hands, broke into the building and ran up the stairs toward our room. One man from our group jumped out of the back window. The gunmen burst into our room. Their leader shouted orders: "Men to the right! Line up against the wall! Women and children to the left and form a line! We know who you dirty deserters are! A bunch of stinking, hiding Jews! We are detectives from the Hungarian Gestapo!"

We thought this was the end. Many prayed. Many sobbed. But nothing happened for a while. About half an hour later the leader of the detectives emerged from the office. He informed us that we were under the protection of the detectives and if we had any trouble we should call them immediately. Then they were gone. All of us were puzzled. What happened? Well, there were some very rich people in our group, and they managed to bribe the detectives with a lot of money.

A few days after this incident it was decided that the twenty children, ranging in age from five months to eleven years, accompanied by the very young mother of a five-month-old baby, should be moved to a building that was under the protection of the International Red Cross. Both my mother and I cried at hearing the news. I had never been away from my mother, even for a day. Only God knew what would happen and when we would see each other again.

The next morning all of us children and the young mother climbed onto a horse-drawn cart, which was driven by the army deserter in uniform. On the way we got caught in an air raid and ran into an underground public shelter. The air raid lasted a long time and was fierce. Afterward, it took us quite a while to reach the Red Cross building.

It was in a very elegant part of Budapest. Before the war, it had been a five-story luxury apartment house. Now the place was run down. A few adults and hundreds of crying, frightened, hungry children jammed the floors. The twenty of us were separated in different parts of the building. John and I were told to join twenty-five to thirty other children of our age in a midsize room. We received no food. There was no furniture in the room. We were told to sleep on the floor. I walked around the apartments. I discovered a friend of mine, Miklós, and his sister in one of the rooms. He told me that they had not eaten for three days. I walked the rooms and corridors, crying. A young girl and her boyfriend saw me. The young man wore the uniform of the Arrow Cross. He told me that the next morning he would take me back to my parents. That really frightened me. If the young man took me to our hiding place, that would be the end of the group.

The next morning I told John that I would escape and try to get back to Csángó Street. He decided to come with me. The outer door of the building was locked. Children could not leave the building without an adult, so we waited until a kind-looking lady came into the building. We asked her if she would take us to buy ourselves some food because we were hungry and had some money. She walked with us, but after a few steps we started to run and lost her. We did not have yellow stars on. We stopped running, fearing that we would draw attention to ourselves. We ducked into buildings whenever we saw an Arrow Cross patrol approaching. Finally, we reached a streetcar station, purchased a newspaper, and climbed aboard the streetcar when it finally arrived. We got off at Csángó Street and walked up to the heavy steel door of the factory. The door opened and in a few minutes I was kissing my crying mother. I told the story of my escape and the conditions in the Red Cross building.

After the war I found out from Miklós (who escaped a day after I did), that three or four days after my escape all the children were taken to the bank of the Danube and machine-gunned into the river by an Arrow Cross group. No one survived.

John and I were the only children in 6 Csángó Street. One of our pastimes was the exploration of the factory building. There were large textile looms in the lower rooms and fascinating huge machines. Some had rolls of loomed material on them and material stretched over the frame. It was fun playing with the "boats." These were elongated hardwood parts with steel tips on both ends. They contained a spool with thread. The "boat" looked like a small canoe.

On December 17, 1944, two policemen knocked on the outer door of the factory. They were let in. The regular police, in general, behaved moderately toward the Jews. These two men told us that our "friends," the detectives, sent them to escort us to the ghetto. They told us that the building across the street from our factory had been the local headquarters of the Arrow Cross for some time, and the people there were growing suspicious of the goings-on in our place. The policemen were very candid with us and told us that they would lead the column to the ghetto and wouldn't look back if some of us decided to just disappear along the way.

My father decided that we would go to the ghetto since we had nowhere else to go. Of the 185 people who started out from the factory only 63 arrived in the ghetto. The policemen were true to their word. They did not look back.

It was a good hour and a half walk from Csángó Street to Klauzál Circle, the center of the ghetto. We entered through the Wesselényi Street entrance. About ten city blocks in Budapest's old and densely populated Jewish section were designated as the ghetto. In it were 162 old apartment houses. The ground floors were occupied by small stores, long abandoned by their owners. At the time we arrived, there were about 63,000 people in that small area. The streets were teeming with mostly old people, women, and children. First we were led to the old market building of Klauzál Circle, where a bunch of young Arrow Cross militiamen told us that we should drop every piece of jewelry, fountain pens, money, and all other valuables into boxes. "You will be subjected to body search and if we find anything on you, you will be executed on the spot," they told us. There were several dead people propped up against the wall of the market building. "They were executed because we found a gold cigarette lighter and some fountain pens on them," said one of the "examiners." Some people from our group threw money and jewelry into the sewer rather than give them to these hooligans. We had nothing.

Their threat of body search did not materialize. We passed through and were led to an adjacent building. The building was packed with old people except on the top level, which had no furniture and was in a terrible condition. Our group was given two rooms in an apartment.

The Jewish ghetto council was looking for volunteers for its "police" force. They defended the ghetto's inhabitants from the Arrow Cross and the SS marauders who came in nightly and raped, robbed, and killed people. The equipment of the "police" force was a night stick. Their uniform consisted of a hard hat, a white armband on which the words "ghetto police" were written in three languages—Hungarian, German, and Russian—and an identification card, also in three languages. They received double food rations as payment and worked on street patrol for twelve hours a day, seven days a week.

My father volunteered—mostly for the food, for me. We were hungry, and the food rations were a plate of watery soup a day. On the second day, my father and I found a piece of moldy bread full of worms. It must have been six months old, but somehow we broke it apart and toasted it. Then, after removing the dead worms, we ate the bread.

Suddenly, at night on the third day of our stay in the ghetto, there was a tremendous explosion followed by a crash. We all jumped up and ran to the windows. The building across from us had been hit by a heavy artillery shell. We heard screams and shouts for help. Many people were dead. I was so frightened that I couldn't stay on the third floor, and I begged my mother to go down to the basement and sleep there. The basement of this old building was deep, dark, and musty. It was the warehouse of a lumber dealer. The dirt floor was covered with three to four inches of sawdust and there were workbenches along the wall. Mother, Kató, who was with us, and I went down to the basement and climbed on a workbench to sleep. We found a short stump of candle that was our only source of light.

The days and nights were filled with noise and explosions. The Russian Army had reached the suburbs, and the siege of Budapest began. Soon everybody from the building had to move into the basement. There was a problem with hygiene. We had one water pipe from which water came in a trickle. (The utility services, such as water, electricity, and gas were nonexistent by the end of December.) There were no toilets either. So the house council decided to dig toilets in the middle of the room and separate them from the rest of us. with torn old bed sheets. The stench was unbearable. Then lice appeared on some people, and because of the close contact the lice spread to all of us.

When the Russian Army completed the encirclement of the city by mid-December, the transports to the deportation camps were halted. There were Jewish forced labor companies trapped in Budapest. Some of them were led into the ghetto. About ten or fifteen of them were brought to our building. They had come largely from the eastern provinces of Hungary. Most of them were very religious. They had been conscripted in 1941 and sent to the Ukraine on the Russian front. They and a few hundred others were the sole survivors of the 70,000 people who were sent there in 1941–42. They knew that their families had been deported. They were skin and bones and survived purely by will. They ate very little and mostly prayed all day long.

Getting our food rations proved to be a very dangerous undertaking. Several people were wounded while carrying food. Volunteers were needed to bring the food to us, and my father was always in this group. They did not want to get killed in the last days of the war.

The new year, 1945, began with very little food and water. We were weak, sitting in the darkness. The only light came from a can of floor wax, which Uncle Joe had found in an abandoned store window. I contributed half of one of my shoelaces. It was pushed into the wax and became the wick of the candle. Uncle Joe was one of the men in the forced labor group. He was in his fifties, a friendly little man. We became friends. I told him that I had this terrific design for a flying submarine, or a submergible airplane, which would have wheels also. You see, before March I had read Jules Verne a lot and was familiar with many of his books, particularly with *Twenty Thousand Leagues Under the Sea*.

There were very few children in the building. I remember only one little girl who was about eight years old. Her name was Alice. She was with her mother, who was a diabetic, and her grandmother. They bunked close to us but were very weak and the girl was sickly, so we didn't play much together. Mostly I was with Uncle Joe.

The days were going fast or slow, I could not really tell. We lost all sense of time. I saw my father every second or third day. Many ghetto policemen were killed by flying shrapnel or by the Nazis who were shooting at everyone who happened to be on the street. My father was on patrol almost all the time. He lost two partners. He was forty-three years old but looked seventy. Except his eyes—they were youthful, alive. One day he came home with good news—he had discovered his parents, my grandparents, in the ghetto.

The days dragged on. More and more of the older people starved to death. We would discover them in the morning. The corpses were taken out of the buildings when there was a lull in the fighting. They were thrown into a large pile in the middle of Klauzál Circle. Hundreds of frozen bodies. There was nobody to bury them. I saw a hill made of human bodies. We knew that if a miracle did not happen soon we would all end up on the hill.

In the middle of January, a young SS soldier came down to our basement. He was surveying our building and told us that the ghetto had been mined.

On January 17, 1945, the sounds of battle were becoming very loud. Artillery duels went on continuously. My father came home and decided to stay overnight. Alice came to my mother and begged for food for her diabetic mother and grandmother. My mother had nothing to give.

On the morning of January 18, 1945, everything was strangely quiet. We climbed up to look through a very small window. Through a crack we could see strange-looking boots—not Nazi boots. They were Russian boots. We were liberated. Alice's mother and grandmother were strangely quiet. They were dead.

We went home to our old apartment on Queen Elizabeth Street, which we had been forced to leave in June of the previous year. My maternal grandmother came home a few hours later. She and all her sisters survived.

Sometime later I found out that the day after we left the factory at Csángó Street it was hit by a bomb and completely destroyed.

Do you believe in miracles? I do!

George Pick graduated from the Jewish High School of Budapest in 1952 and studied mechanical engineering at the Technical University of Budapest. He left Hungary during the Revolution of 1956 and settled in the United States. He received his M.S. in mechanical engineering from the Catholic University in Washington, D.C., in 1962 and taught there as an assistant professor. Since then he has been employed by the U.S. Navy as a senior staff engineer and engineering manager. Presently he is the technical director of the Navy's NATO Seasparrow Project Office. He lives in the Washington metropolitan area.

ANDRÉ STEIN

THE BIRTHDAY SURPRISE

It was 1942, and this particular day was to be the most splendid day of my life. What little boy would not have been thrilled to spend his sixth birthday on a country estate in the middle of the mystical Great Plain of Hungary? And if you add to this the fact that I had never left the part of Budapest called "Chicago," you'd agree that it was going to be a glorious adventure. My parents kept dropping mysterious hints: "There will be all kinds of surprises, you'll see." But they refused to say more. All I knew about this special day was that we were going to spend it at my father's cousin's country estate. And even if it hadn't been my birthday, it promised to be the most exciting day ever.

You see, Uncle Alex was a veterinarian and a gentleman farmer. At night, when I closed my eyes, instead of sleeping, I daydreamed about all the animals I'd not only get to see up close but also to touch. In the darkness of the small room that my parents, my sister, Agi, and I shared day and night, I gave my imagination complete freedom. I conjured up tiger cubs and their protective mothers, mammoth-size elephants blowing circles in the dark dust of the Great Plain. I even shivered with delicious fright as my fantasy wandered onto the image of a menacing king cobra. How would all these tropical beasts land on my uncle's estate in central Hungary? Well, six-year olds—Hungarians, Americans, or Chinese—have one thing in common: they have their own ideas about where to find what in the world.

I was so caught up in my daydreaming about the journey and the visit that I didn't even think about the birthday gifts I would be receiving, or for that matter, if I was going to get anything at all. It was a most spectacular present that I was going to be in another world—one that had nothing in common with the dirty, dangerous streets where I lived—a world in which I didn't have to worry about the barefoot brats who kept calling me a "rotten Jewish bedbug." I was going to travel! Like an explorer! It made no difference that the train ride would take no more than a few hours. I was going to cherish every moment and make each one of them last forever.

"Sit on the coal bin, my boy, and just be quiet," Mother said to me time and time again. "Play in peace, there is no space for horseplaying in a tiny apartment like ours. You'll have every chance in the world to run around to your heart's content in the country with your little cousins. But if you don't calm down, we may just have to cancel the whole trip."

"Oh how cruel parents can be," I sighed with resignation, perched on the hard wooden bin in our windowless kitchen. It was a hopeless place, except when Mother was preparing some goodie whose aroma allowed my nose to take me on fabulous journeys of sumptuous feasts in princely palaces. "In fact, everything and everybody is mean and cruel. But the worst of it is time: it seems to have slowed down just to torment me." Even Agi, who was eleven and was sweet and quiet most of the time, devoting all her attention to her china doll, kept teasing me with comments like, "Are you trying to grow wings and fly ahead of the rest of us?" or, "If you don't calm down, we might have to scrape you off the ceiling. And you don't even know about the watermelons."

And, in spite of the snail's pace of the old alarm clock, July 28 finally dawned. We dressed with my parents' usual calm. Mother inspected my fingernails just to be sure that she wasn't going to be ashamed of me in front of all the relatives. She dressed me in an outfit that she had just finished sewing the night before. Dad was shining my Sunday lace-up boots. Nothing seemed to be more important to Dad than the shine on one's shoes. "Show me your shoes, and I'll tell you who you are," he said every Sunday as he polished every pair of shoes in the house.

Loaded with packages, we closed the kitchen door behind us. I cast a final glance at the dark kitchen. I *knew* that I was going to be part of something so extraordinary that it was going to change me forever. So I wanted to make sure that I could fix in my mind once and for all what my tiny world looked like before the "event."

We walked to the nearby Eastern Railroad Station. I carried a small knapsack on my back. If it had been filled with diamonds, I couldn't have felt prouder. "Look at Shitty Steven, he is so decked-out it must be his birthday," one of the barefoot brats yelled at me as he spat only a foot away from me. I looked at Dad, hoping that he'd grab the brat by the ear and make him lick up his own saliva on the dusty sidewalk. But Dad wasn't interested at all. "Is your name Steven? No, it isn't, so don't pay attention to what is not your business," he said quietly, without even looking at me.

To anyone accustomed to country landscapes, my train ride would have been a terrible bore. But I found the rapidly appearing and disappearing images fascinating. I was startled when Mother whispered into my ear, "If you don't close your mouth, your stomach will catch a draft." It seemed that each time I blinked there was a new pasture, or a cornfield, or wheatfields. These scenes of a nature tamed by farmers were interrupted here and there by tiny farmhouses, or a cozy village huddled around a church steeple. How I would have loved to abandon our gray "Chicago," unadorned by any vegetation, for the open green fields and the tree-lined streets of these quaint villages.

The wheels came to a screeching stop. I was jolted back into reality. The train was in a small station. The sign above the head of the important-looking old stationmaster read "KISHALAS." We had arrived.

I jumped up as if the seat had caught on fire. Everybody laughed at me. "There is plenty of time, my boy," Father said with a superior smile, flashing his row of gold teeth. "There are all these people ahead of us." Most of the people in our train car were dressed in folk costumes. The men were clad in black and white, many of them sporting gray handlebar moustaches, and most of the women had dark kerchiefs wrapped around their shoulders, drawn tightly at their waists. But my eyes were riveted on their ample skirts, which revealed many layers of starched petticoats. When the women made even the slightest movement, the petticoats seemed to take on a life of their own.

Uncle Alex's horse-drawn carriage was waiting for us at the station. His estate was about three kilometers (2 mi) away. To my great pleasure, the tall, massive horse, Csillag, was not about to break any speed records, so the journey was just as slow-paced as I would have wanted it to be. I kept staring at Csillag's brown-and-white speckled rear end. Its slow sway reminded me of the petticoats worn by the peasant women on the train.

By the time Csillag came to a stop, we were in front of the imposing white stucco home of our relatives. There were a lot of them to greet us. In fact, we were the last arrivals. In addition to Uncle Alex's three children and his wife, Aunt Lili, there was my cousin Tomi. He was a year older than I, and he was known as a first-class daredevil. There was also cousin Vera, the ballerina. I never saw her dance, but I had to admit that she was the most beautiful girl I had ever seen. And there were, of course, Mother's sisters, Manci and Ila, and their husbands. I don't remember much about my uncles except that they had a most peculiar way of speaking, not like the rest of us. I was sure that my two uncles had a dark secret that was responsible for their weird way of speaking Hungarian.

It was Uncle Nathan who lifted me out of the carriage. He picked me up by the waist and threw me in the air as high as he could while shouting with fake anxiety in his voice, "My God, I hope I can catch him."

And there was Grandmother also, of course. She was Mother's fat, selfish mother, with a head like a hairy cabbage. I never liked her because she always competed with us children. Her eager eyes were always on the lookout to see if one of us was eating a special treat. I quickly picked up from my older cousins and Agi that when Grandmother was around we'd better hide our goodies, or we'd pay dearly. No wonder she was fat enough to take up two seats on the streetcar.

"Kati, take the children to their quarters," Uncle Alex ordered the young servant girl. "While I attend to the neighbor's mare's aches and pains, they can freshen up before dinner. Today, you children will have an early night because tomorrow is the BIG DAY and we have things to do."

We were ushered through the large house, passing through a dark hallway. On either side, there were huge rooms with the blinds all the way down to keep out the stifling July heat of the Great Plain. I was amazed by the number of rooms. I had never been in a home that had more than three rooms altogether. Before we had reached the door at the end of the vast corridor, I had counted six rooms. Each one had beds in it. To me, who shared one room with my parents and my sister, it just didn't make sense. Why would everybody want to have his own room? "Don't they get lonesome at night, or frightened when there is a strange noise or a mysterious wind blowing?" I whispered to Agi. "The rich are never frightened," she whispered back. For the first time in my life, I wished I were rich. Because I was frightened a lot.

The four of us cousins shared a very large room, and I was very happy to have my cousins and my big sister in the same room with me. When Mother blew out the flame in the oil lamp, I swallowed a big gulp of air in fright. I had never been in such a deep darkness as the one that enveloped our room. At home, here and there, a street light would sneak into our room by the edge of the cloth blind Father rolled down every night. Or I could catch a glimpse of the moon on a clear night.

"Out of bed, lazy bones," Uncle Alex's cheery voice woke me the next morning. "Did I really sleep?" was my first thought. It seemed to me that I had spent the whole night waiting for this moment. It was the first sound that I heard as a six year old.

If my life depended on it, I couldn't recall what I had for breakfast or in whose company. "Well, first things first," Father said with a sneaky smile on his usually serious face. Father was looking at me, at Agi, then at Tomi, and finally at Vera, the four heroes of the day. Mother walked to the hutch by the wall and returned with four of the biggest chocolate boxes I have ever seen. Agi, as the oldest, got the first one: a red heart-shaped one. Vera got a pink round one. Tomi's was a green square box. Finally, Father winked at me and with a hardly noticeable nod he signalled to me to go to Mother for my gift.

"Happy Birthday, young man," Mother said trying to look serious. After all, she wasn't speaking to a kid, she called me a "young man" for the first time ever. I felt myself grow a foot. That was my very first and most precious birthday surprise. Then came the box of chocolates. It was not only the biggest ever but it was also superbly purple. And the box was oblong. Naturally, I wanted to rip it open at once and feast my eyes and mouth on a sea of different pieces of chocolate. "Patience, my son," Father said, putting his hand on the lid, "everything in its own time. We don't eat candy at the breakfast table, not even on our birthday. It'll wait until dinner."

That was the lowest blow! I looked around the table to see if someone would come to my rescue. But no one seemed interested in convincing Father that one of the best things about birthdays is that everyday rules don't apply. Instead, all the grown-ups nodded silently, like so many judges saying "Guilty, chop his head off." Grandmother was the only one who looked disappointed. She, too, was gypped of the few pieces of chocolate which would have been graciously offered to her, had we been allowed to tear into our treasure chests.

"Well then I'll go to our room and hide my box myself," I said defiantly. I wanted to exercise *some* power over my life. What's the point of being a "young man" if one has to go on doing only what one is told to do? Without waiting for anyone's permission I ran to the children's room and I hid the box under my blanket, giving it a gentle pat. "I'll be back, don't worry," I whispered.

After breakfast we all went outside. The grown-ups were busy whispering about something. First, I thought it had to do with the next surprise of the birthday party. But when I looked closer, I saw that the women looked pale, the men's faces seemed darker and wrinkled. "We're all sitting ducks here," I caught Uncle Imre's voice. "I think we should kiss the kids and all of us scatter—like birds when they smell the cat coming."

"You, over there, you come with me," Uncle Alex shouted at me, making a hook with his index finger as if he wanted to grab me with it. "I'll show you some of my patients before we head for the fields."

He didn't have to repeat the invitation. I was most eager to see his "beasts." I was mildly disappointed to see only a couple of horses, a donkey, and a very tired looking old Puli dog. No exotic animals, no mysterious creatures. "You can come closer, they are very nice. Here all creatures are used to being gentle because we are gentle to them. You can even pet them."

I grew a little shy, but I did take a few steps closer, close enough to pet the donkey on the furthest part from his big yellow teeth. My sister was playing with the old Puli dog that looked like it had long black ropes instead of hair.

"Oh, you dirty old rascal," I heard Uncle Alex yell. That was the first time I'd heard him raise his voice. When I turned around I saw that the shirt on his back was all wet. His three kids and Vera, who saw what happened, were twisted into all kinds of shapes from laughter.

"The old mare peed on Papa when he climbed under her

to check her tummy," Peti, his oldest son shouted, loud enough to alert the entire county. I was angry at having been robbed of seeing with my own eyes this most bizarre event, something no one would ever believe and which I couldn't swear to because I didn't really see it happen.

A few minutes later, however, Uncle Alex was outside again in a fresh shirt. "Well, I deserved what I got for trying to work on such a special day," he said cheerfully. "But, you city folks should know that a country veterinarian has no days off. Now it's time for more important business. Everyone follow me—the four guests of honor come right up front."

The whole company set out toward the fields. We walked for quite awhile under the burning sun. There was no surprise in sight. My mood was beginning to cloud over when suddenly we came to a stop. I opened my eyes and all I saw was a thick row of green stalks aiming at the sky. "Look at the top," Uncle Alex said as if he had read my mind.

I looked skyward. What I saw was worth craning my neck for: sunflowers. But not just any old sunflowers. Sunflowers that seemed as big as bicycle wheels. The shortest stalk was much taller than the tallest of my uncles. Uncle Alex climbed up a ladder to harvest four of those huge flowers. He handed one to each of the birthday heroes. I had a hard time carrying mine. "You might need a hand with that, my son," Father said. But I would rather have dragged it on all fours than let go of this most extraordinary gift. "It must have a million seeds," I exclaimed. "I dare you to count them," Aunt Manci teased me.

"You may all hide your sunflowers under the plants. They'll be waiting for you on the way back. But hide them well, otherwise the birds will have a royal feast while we're gone."

After we put our bounty in the shade of the tall stalks, we followed Uncle Alex toward the field—all except Grandmother. "This heat and all this walking is a bit too much for my old bones. I'll head back and catch a wink or two on the veranda," she said.

We must have walked for another ten minutes before Uncle Alex stopped. I saw nothing worthy of attention, just the leaves of some plants that seemed to be growing out of the ground, lying quite lazily. "Certainly they could hide no worthwhile secret," I thought. But boy was I wrong!

There was a spade waiting in front of each plant. Uncle Alex posted each one of us in front of one of them and said: "Start digging, kids. Mother Earth has a surprise for each one of you." So I started digging. It was only a matter of a minute before the blade hit something hard.

"The rest you'll have to do with your hands," Uncle Alex cautioned me, "otherwise you'll crack the surprise." I dropped to my knees and dug into the dirt fiercely with my fingers. I felt like a dog sniffing out a buried bone.

And there it was, the surprise of my life! If a genie had jumped out of a bottle I couldn't have been more amazed. It was a small but perfectly shaped round watermelon. What was so special about a watermelon, one might be tempted to ask. Well, it grew with my name in its dark rind. It grew just for me. I couldn't believe my eyes. The earth grew something just for me! Can there be anything more special than that? After the first shock let up a bit, I looked at my cousins and my sister: they all had their own watermelons with their names in the rinds, too. If I had been turned into an old bearded goat at that moment, I would have been satisfied with having lived an extraordinary moment.

"Well, we should get going," Uncle Nathan said. Was it his strange way of speaking Hungarian or was there really a hint of worry in his voice? His comment gave me a sinking feeling that not everything was going to be wonderful about this day. I looked at the grown-ups and I saw worry written all over their faces.

We began to walk back to the house. We did what comes naturally to kids. We ran around, just as Mother had predicted back in our dark kitchen when she made me sit on the coal bin. We chased each other, we played catch, and we made a lot of noise. Wherever we went flocks of birds took flight.

When we turned around the corner of the large white house that was Uncle Alex's family home and office, we all went "Aaaah!" What we saw was a magnificent table set in the courtyard for the whole family. It was laden with shiny white china, dazzling silver flatware, and sparkling glasses on a table cloth white as fresh snow. There were flowers and wine flasks and huge loaves of golden egg breads the like of which I only saw on the High Holy Days.

I felt very special. After all, I was one of the four guests of honor. "All right, children," I heard Aunt Lili's cheerful voice beckon to us, "wash up quickly because lunch is not going to wait for you." I ran into the house to do as I was told. Then I remembered the purple box of chocolates. I just couldn't resist the urge to take a quick peek at my treasure.

I ran to my bed in the children's room and reached under the bedspread to pull out the box. But my hands found absolutely nothing. I was horrified. I reached under the covers once more to search for my chocolate box, this time more thoroughly. Still nothing. I was in a state of panic. It was like a horrible nightmare. I threw the covers back. There was not a thing on the spotless white sheet. SOMEBODY STOLE MY PURPLE OBLONG BOX OF CHOCOLATES! And I never even had a chance to taste one piece; I never even had a chance to take a peek at what was in the box. This was the most cruel thing a person could do to me. "I have never been so unhappy in my life," I thought as I stood by the empty bed with tears bathing my face, "and I'll never be unhappier even if I live forever."

"What in the world is the matter?" I heard Mother's voice from my bedroom door. I could have been standing there crying for five minutes or for five hours, I had lost all sense of time. "My goodness, what has happened here?" said Mother, holding me by the shoulder very gently. She, too, sounded upset. Well, as if I had been waiting just for this signal, I started to cry with my whole body. I shook from head to toe; it felt as if I had tears coming from every pore of my skin. Not a word could come out of my mouth. Mother was trying her best to calm me down, but nothing worked, not even her best caresses or even her best bribes. She ran out of the room yelling. "Something dreadful has happened to our boy. Alex, come help me." Both Uncle Alex and Father came running—which makes good sense, because Father's name was Alex, also.

"It's quite simple, dreadful but simple," Father said as soon as he had seen the bare bed. "His box of chocolates is missing. That's where he hid it before we all left for the fields."

"All except the servant girl, Kati," Uncle Alex said in a dark voice. I imagined lightning was going to strike a second after he spoke. "That good-for-nothing brat was the only one left in the house, she had to be the one who stole the kid's chocolates. Well, I'll see to this at once. I won't tolerate thieves in my home. And you, young man, you'll get most of your chocolate back immediately, or you can call me Black Peter from here on." Black Peter wasn't a real person, but everyone hated him all the same: he was an imaginary creature who turned everything good into evil.

"You ungrateful little thief, you return to my nephew his chocolate box at once, or I'll make belts out of the skin on your back," I heard Uncle Alex's thundering voice from the hallway. A minute or two later he appeared in the frame of the door, dragging the terrified servant girl by the ear.

"I never touched his box," she sobbed, "I never even knew he hid it in here or anywhere, I never laid eyes on his chocolates, may God strike me dead on this spot if I'm lying. You've got to believe me, Doctor."

"You were the only one who remained behind, you had to be the one." Uncle Alex tightened his hold on Kati's ear. The poor girl was writhing in pain and fear. "It's not enough that you steal, on top of it you lie and blaspheme. Where did you hide the box, you wretched creature? Out with the truth or out with you. You can go back to your mother. I won't keep you in the same house with my children." Then he turned toward us: "I looked everywhere in her room but there was no trace of chocolates. But there are a million and one places to hide a box of chocolates on this estate." Once again, he turned toward the girl: "This is your last chance to confess or you can leave my house at once and I will hold back your week's wages and I will sell all your things in the county fair to raise the money for another box of chocolates. So it's up to you to decide."

He let go of her ear. She rubbed it gently as she stood there like a beaten dog. I began to feel sorry for her. I was about to say something about not caring about the chocolates anymore when I saw her straighten up and look Uncle Alex in the eye like an equal:

"I have never stolen as much as a pin from you or anyone, may lightning strike me on this spot if I am lying. But since you, sir, refuse to believe me, I'll leave your house, but you'll be sorry one day to have accused an innocent person so cruelly. You'll be sorry." And she ran out as fast as she could.

"Well, I don't much want to believe that she did it," Uncle Alex said, shaken by what had happened. "I've known her ever since she was a baby. In a way, she was a member of the family. But sometimes the best person can do a bad thing. This is a most disturbing surprise for you, my boy, and for my family. But don't worry, I'll get you another box of chocolates tomorrow. In the meantime, let's return to the table. We still have a wonderful feast waiting for us. And in the afternoon . . . I was going to keep it a secret, but seeing that our birthday boy is rather green at the edges, I may as well let the cat out of the bag. All the kids are going for a ride to the pond for a glorious afternoon of swimming."

That did it for me. Swimming in the pond! I'd never been in a pond. What an incredible adventure. If my chocolates hadn't been stolen, this would have been the best birthday a six-year-old ever had.

When we returned to the table, everyone sat without moving a muscle, without blinking an eye, without whispering a sound. "How dreadful that she stole your chocolates," Agi whispered to me when I sat down next to her. "I'll share mine with you." "How did you know what happened?" I whispered back. "Nobody came in and nobody left the house, so how does everyone know?" "Kati came running out and she told us all that she was sent away because Uncle Alex accused her of stealing your birthday gift but she took nothing and that we will all be sorry for the wrong that was done to her on this cursed day. Aunt Lili said she ran toward the town—which was curious, because her mother lives in the opposite direction."

By this time the chilled sour cherry soup in my bowl was more interesting to me. Nothing would make my chocolates come back, but in the meantime sour cherry soup happened to be my favorite summer food. The whole meal was a feast the like of which I have never seen, even in a storybook. When I finished the last piece of poppyseed strudel, I thought my belly would burst.

The afternoon was another fairy tale. Swimming in a pond was nothing like swimming in a crowded, smelly swimming pool. I had never been in the water with all kinds of little fishes. And the water was so clear that I could see my feet without sticking my face into it. We swam and we played "fish," "catch," and water polo. The ride back was a lot of fun, too. We had two buggies for the seven of us kids. Uncle Alex and Father followed us in their own sulky. We sang so loud all the way home that we were probably heard all around the Great Plain.

When we arrived back at the house, the grown-ups seemed even more serious than before. My two aunts and their husbands were all dressed in their city clothes, and their packed bags were standing on the veranda.

"Ila, Manci, boys, stay at least for supper," Aunt Lili was begging them. "Once we eat, Alex will drive you to the evening train, and no harm will have been done. Don't end your children's birthday on a note of gloom." My two aunts looked at each other, then at their husbands. Their husbands murmured something in a language I had never heard. Uncle Nathan threw his arms in the air as if to say: Do what you want to do, I don't care anymore.

They all stayed for supper. In order for them to have plenty of time to catch the train, we ate earlier than usual. Since Kati had been sent away, Aunt Lili and the other women served the food.

But by then I was ready to go to sleep. The day had been so full of events that I felt "wrung out like a dish towel" as Mother used to say at the end of her workdays. I wanted to go to bed and recall every little detail that had happened to me, to make sure that nothing would be left out when, later, I would want to relive this extraordinary birthday. I still felt very hurt about my birthday chocolates being stolen. Not only because they were a fabulous gift, but because somebody had taken what belonged to me. Somebody didn't care about hurting my feelings.

Dinner was a fantastic choice of cold dishes: salamis, sausages, cheeses, deviled eggs, and salads, served with still-warm country bread. But by the time Mother put a plateful in front of me, my eyes were half closed.

"Oh, my God," I heard Mother whisper. A quick glance at her face made it clear that she had just seen a most frightening thing. All eyes followed her gaze toward the front gate. We all froze in silent terror. Two *pandur* (a kind of county police) had appeared on bicycle. There was indeed nothing more terrifying on earth than pandurs. And now they were here. And without a word, they were approaching the company.

We were silent like graves in a cemetery. "Kati," Aunt Lili whispered.

"We came to check your company's papers, Doctor," one of them said to Uncle Alex. He didn't sound particularly mean, but he didn't sound friendly, either. "It appears that you are entertaining some foreign Jews, Polish perhaps."

"Everyone you see around this table is a member of my family, Miklós," Uncle Alex said softly, looking the pandur right in the eyes. "And everyone who is under my roof is sitting around this table. Whoever told you otherwise was either ill informed or wanted to harm us. Have a glass of wine to the good health of our four birthday heroes and return to the town in peace." Without waiting for the pandur's reply he filled two glasses with red wine and handed them to the two silent lawmen.

"We are on official business, Doctor," Miklós answered. "We'll toast another time. Now, if you please, we want to see the papers of all your guests." The other pandur just stood behind, without a word, watching what was happening. Every once in a while he took a glance around the table to make sure everyone was still there.

"Where do you think you are going?" he yelled at Uncle Nathan who stood up and began to walk toward the house. The pandur raised his bayonet-mounted rifle just a bit as if he wanted to remind everyone of his power over life and death.

"His documents are . . ." Aunt Manci answered before my uncle could open his mouth. But the pandur stopped her with a cold outburst of anger: "Did I ask anything of you? Can't he speak for himself? Is he dumb?" Then he turned to my uncle again. "Where do you think you are going? Answer when a man of law asks you an official question, for God's sake!"

"I'm going to fetch my papers inside the house," my uncle's voice sounded as if it came from a deep cave. It sounded even more foreign than usual.

"Corporal, listen to this man massacring our beautiful language," the pandur yelled to his superior. "This one has just spoken his document. If he isn't one of those Polish Jews I'll eat the feathers in my cap." With a sudden jerk, he took his rifle off his shoulder and pointed it at my uncle. Uncle Nathan seemed to have turned to a pillar of salt. He couldn't move, his face was as waxy as a candle.

"All right, Jew, step to the side. His wife and children join him at once," sounded the crisp order. Aunt Manci and Vera stood up slowly and properly, and walked over to Uncle Nathan's side, hand in hand.

"Anyone else . . ." the corporal started to bark at the rest of us at the table, but before he could finish his sentence, Uncle Simon was already on his feet and without being told, he walked over to the others. Without a word, Aunt Ila picked up Tomi in her arms and she followed her husband.

"And what about you, what are you waiting for?" the corporal snapped at Father. "You need a written invitation or what?"

"My grandfather was Hungarian, my father was Hungarian, and therefore I am Hungarian, too. Just as you are,"

Father said, looking the pandur straight in the eye. He didn't even rise to his feet. I was never so proud of Father.

"Well, not quite," the pandur snapped back, "Hungarian or not, you're nothing but a Jew. Your day will come, too, I promise. For now, your papers before I get angry."

Without haste, Father handed over our papers, which he had already prepared while waiting for his turn. He definitely had things under control. And the pandur didn't seem to like that at all.

"A wise guy, aren't you, Jew?" He moved close to Father and poked him hard with his finger. "I could take you in just for contempt of the law, but for the time being, you can thank me for just a warning. There won't be a second time. Pack your things, and you and your gang beat it out of here and never come back." To mark his words, he spit on the ground. His spit landed just short of Father's shoes.

"The rest of you law-breakers, move it out, we have some distance to cover before the sun sets." And he motioned with his rifle to my aunts, uncles, and cousins to start marching toward the gate. Uncle Nathan made a move toward the veranda where the bags were standing.

"Never mind your garbage," the pandur said, shoving him back into the line. "You won't need anything. It would be just a burden to carry. You'll have everything you need where you are all going."

One pandur at the head of the line, and one at the tail, they all marched out. The rest of us sat like statues. Grandmother was the only one who was muttering a prayer in Hebrew. Then I noticed something. As she reached into a pocket to pull out a handkerchief to wipe the tears and the sweat off her face, she pulled out a crumbled shiny silver paper along with her handkerchief. Just the kind that chocolates are usually wrapped in! I froze in terror. I wanted to scream but no voice came out of my mouth.

So it was *her*, my fat, greedy grandmother, and not Kati. The poor servant girl got sent away and she was shamed. And all the time it was my grandmother who couldn't stand being left out when the treats were handed out. I felt so confused and so much hatred for her as I looked in the direction

INDEX

Air raids, 21, 22, 29, 36, 39–40, 53, 54, 62, 70, 72–73, 75, 105, 106, 107–108, 110, 124, 125–127
Albertfalva, 90–91, 93
Arrow Cross Party, 33, 128
Arrow Cross troops, 22, 23, 75, 85, 86, 92, 97, 130
Auschwitz, 71, 83, 116

Barta, Peter, 85–94
Bauer, Tibor, 95–113
Bratislava, 112
Budapest, 21–22, 28, 43, 45
    bombing of, 126–127

Christians, assuming identity of, 22, 62–65
Curfew, 125, 130

Debrecen, 95–96, 111, 113

Escapes, 38–39, 45–47, 62–65, 129–131

Firing squads, 23, 34, 77, 119, 134
Food shortage, 24, 25, 36, 48, 71–72, 76, 78, 80, 100, 101
Fumigating chamber, 101–102

German occupation, 22, 27–28, 42, 44, 52, 60, 70, 73, 85, 115, 128–129
Ghetto, 20–21, 33–34, 53, 54, 80, 98, 116–117, 119, 135–139
Ghetto police force, 136, 138
Great Plain, 141, 142, 145
Gunskirchen, 83

Hajdúszoboszló, 63–65
Handler, Andrew, 57–66
Hanoar Ha-Zioni, 82
Hentz, Martha, 51–55
Hitler Youth organization, 61
Horthy, Miklós, 32–33
Houses, Nazi seizure of, 22, 28, 31–32, 54, 66

Identification papers, fakes, 22–23, 33, 63, 116
Illness, 79, 81, 90, 92
Ipolysag, 93–94

Kalman, Gabor, 19–25
Kalocsa, 19–20, 25
Kishalas, 144
Klauzál Circle, 135, 138

Labor camps, 29, 36, 52, 62, 71, 81, 103–104, 115, 125

Living quarters of Jews, 24, 29, 34–35, 36, 45, 47, 53, 63, 73–74, 85, 89, 96, 124–125, 132–133

Marshal law, 128–129
Mauthausen, 83
Meschel, Susan V., 67–84
Milch, Peter O., 27–40
Muszosok, 88

Óbuda, 58, 66, 73, 91
Óbuda Brickyard, 91–93

Pets, selling as meat, 72
Pick, George S., 123–139
Possessions, hiding of, 70–71, 82, 97, 100
Protective papers nature of, 116
   See also Identification papers

Raids on Jews, 21, 22, 23, 33–34, 37–40, 52, 73, 74–75, 77, 86–91, 116, 155–158
Red Cross orphanage, 117, 133–134
Roadblocks, 21

Russian liberation, 22, 37, 48, 54, 65, 78–81, 108, 111–113, 118–119, 136–139

School, after the liberation, 82
Schoolchildren, attacks on, 19–20, 23, 42–43, 52
SS officers, 20, 21
Star of David, 20, 32, 33, 61, 73, 104, 124–125, 129
Stein, André, 141–158
Swedish protection, 92–94, 118, 132
Swiss house, 34–35, 47, 73–74, 116
Swiss Letters of Protection, 33
Székely, Éva, 41–49

Tarjan, Peter, 115–121
Trains, to transport Jews, 99–101, 109

Vienna, 102–108

Wallenberg, Raoul, 118, 119, 120–121, 132

Zionist underground, 76, 82